THE GRADUATE
RECRUITMENT MANUAL

The Graduate Recruitment Manual

Rajvinder Kandola
Robert Wood
Bindi Dholakia
Carol Keane

Gower

Published by
Gower Publishing Limited
Gower House
Croft Road
Aldershot
Hampshire GU11 3HR
England

Gower Publishing Company
131 Main Street
Burlington, VT 05401-5600 USA

British Library Cataloguing in Publication Data
The graduate recruitment manual
   1. College graduates – Employment – Great Britain
   I. Kandola, Rajvinder II. Pearn Kandola Occupational
Psychologists
331.1'1423'0941

ISBN 0 566 08023 0

Library of Congress Cataloging-in-Publication Data
The graduate recruitment manual / by Rajvinder Kandola . . . [et al.].
     p. cm
  ISBN 0-566-08023-0 (hardcover)
   1. College graduates–Employment–Great Britain. 2. College
students–Employment–Great Britain. 3. Graduate
students–Employment–Great Britain.
   4. Employees–Recruiting–Great Britain.   I. Kandola, R. S.

HD6278.G7 G69 2001
658.3'111–dc21   00-053564

Typeset in Sabon by IML Typographers, Birkenhead, Merseyside
and printed in Great Britain by TJ International Ltd., Padstow, Cornwall.

Contents

Figures and tables

Acknowledgements

Thanks to Jane Beresford for the use of the research on induction reported in Chapter 9. Under the terms of its liaison with the Institute of Work Psychology, University of Sheffield, Pearn Kandola sponsored Jane to do this work as part of her MSc thesis.

Warm thanks go to Niki Manning and Stevie Heath at Pearn Kandola for their help in putting the manuscript together. Julia Scott at Gower has been most supportive in seeing the book through.

Leadership / Focus gaps

Competencies first

measure current against areas

fill gap

Design:

MBA's

Interns:

Placements

Work Experience

Flexible modular programming

supported by major focus led by sessions led by senior mgt

Ask what they're head about dev programmes/learning

mix don't eat

OD – Scope – aut the input + output, process too?

dept

Introduction

If you are recruiting graduates, you are first and foremost dipping into a convenient pool of well-educated people. These people are predominantly young, although there are more mature students than there used to be, and they bring something different to the pool. But what all graduates share is a promising future. Well-educated with futures – that's good news. And employers recognize this. A survey from Income Data Services early in 2000 reported that big employers planned to take on 25 per cent more graduates in 2000 than in 1999.

As a category of recruitment, graduate recruitment is unique. The population of people to be selected from is quite homogeneous; it is relatively easy to define and access. Organizations are in direct competition with one another to select from this pool, and they make strenuous efforts via the milk-round to look at this pool at locations which are convenient to the graduates themselves. In requiring graduates to apply to their websites (as more and more companies are doing) they can rely on them to have the necessary savvy.

Much has been written on the different aspects of graduate recruitment – recruitment, selection, image, expectations (on both sides) – but graduate recruiters have never been able to find it all in one place. By pulling together these different strands, this book offers a kaleidoscopic view of graduate recruitment – from competencies to recruitment, selection, induction and retention.

While writing this book, we have undertaken literature reviews of the relevant research as well as conducting several original pieces of research ourselves. This research has enabled us to look at graduate recruitment from both sides: the employer and the graduate. We asked organizations what they are doing and we asked students what they thought of what organizations do. We went further and asked students what kind of organizations they wanted to work for. This gave us valuable insights into how organizations present themselves and the messages they are putting across and getting across, knowingly or unknowingly.

Induction is what happens to individuals when they join an organization. Would it surprise you to know that relatively little time is spent on it? A feature of this book is the attention we give to induction, again using our own sponsored research. Get induction wrong and bang goes retention. You have lost for good one of these well-educated people with a future. Get induction right – you may still lose people, but it's important to get it right.

The book is about graduate recruitment, selection, induction and retention. It is meant for all graduate recruiters, but anyone who recruits professionally should get something out of it. We would also like to think that students and academics would find something of value in the book, although it is deliberately not an academic treatment. The most technical it gets is in Chapter 6 but that material will not bother anyone who does recruitment daily. Above all, the book is intended for global use in keeping with the theme and content of Chapter 7. Our context may be the UK but given adjustments for local variation we believe the book has universal application.

You will want to know what each chapter contains.

Curious about how graduate recruitment is changing? **Chapter 1** will tell you. It looks at some of the fundamental changes taking place. These include the structure and growth of tertiary education, the composition of the graduate population, and the demand for graduates. It examines and explores issues such as what graduates and recruiters expect of each other. An important factor in all of this – cost – is also discussed.

Worried about your image? Read **Chapter 2**. It examines how corporate images work in attracting applicants of the appropriate quality. The message an organization sends out and the way it is interpreted by potential applicants is a critical factor in determining whether recruitment is going to be effective and successful. We explore what organizations can do to improve their image to graduates.

What do graduates themselves think about organizations? Find out in **Chapter 3**. It looks at the current practice of graduate recruitment and selection in organizations and what students think of the process. If it is the case that students generally dislike, say, personality questionnaires, or being asked to do several interviews, then you need to be aware of this. You might not, as some might say, 'pander' to them, but you will be sensible to keep the knowledge in your head.

Concerned that you are not attracting graduates from ethnic minorities (or enough of them)? If so, you will find **Chapter 4** instructive. It takes a problem that has been voiced by many organizations, namely the failure to attract ethnic minorities, and attempts to locate the causes. We present the findings of original research looking at differences between white and ethnic minority students in terms of what they are looking for in an employer. The most significant finding, perhaps, is that there *are* differences. We explore what these differences mean to employers and how they might respond to them.

Getting the right applicants to apply and the wrong applicants not to apply is key to any sound recruitment drive. **Chapter 5** goes into what to do.

Chapter 6 looks at the different stages involved in building an effective selection process. The pros and cons of each selection method are summarized and constructive suggestions made as to what particular combinations of methods organizations might want to use.

What type(s) of graduate recruitment are you likely to be in? If you are one of the many companies going global, you face particular issues, for instance, how to find culturally fair selection methods. **Chapter 7** goes into the issues.

Then there is the sometimes vexed question of high flyers: who are they, how do you find them, what do you do with them, how do you keep them? **Chapter 8** answers these questions.

Heard about induction but doing nothing about it? Read **Chapter 9.** It goes beyond recruitment to *induction*, that early period a graduate spends with a new organization. Is it sensible to spend large sums of money putting together a smart recruitment campaign to recruit graduates, and then neglect them once you have them?

After induction – what next? Having recruited and inducted, you now need to retain. **Chapter 10** deals with the way graduates are managed and looks at three issues: the manager–graduate relationship? developing graduates? and how to retain graduates.

You will want some best practice standards for easy reference. The **Appendix** provides them. These standards can be used directly to audit your own processes, or help you design your own.

The new context of graduate recruitment

The last ten years have seen the context of graduate recruitment change fundamentally, and forever. There have been changes in:

- the structure and growth of tertiary education
- the composition of the graduate population
- the demand for graduates
- graduates' expectations of employers
- employers' expectations of graduates
- the costs of graduate recruitment.

To this list must be added the globalization of graduate recruitment, an issue considered in Chapter 7.

The structure and growth of tertiary education

In 1992, the Further Education and Higher Education Acts abolished the distinction between universities and polytechnics. The impact was momentous: the ex-polytechnics immediately attracted increased student fee revenue and, without exactly displacing the top institutions, very soon became a force to be reckoned with.

A radical overhaul of the traditional degree classification system also took place in the '90s. For some time, graduates have been emerging from higher education with credits earned in various modules and an overall report describing their achievements.

Students used to have their tuition fees paid by the state. No longer, except in Scotland where, as long as they stay in Scotland, Scottish students will enjoy fee concessions which will relieve them of the burden of up-front tuition fees. Also gone are hardship grants, except in deserving cases. Doom and gloom merchants predicted that from 1997 (when tuition fees were introduced) student numbers would fall dramatically but the latest figures from UCAS indicate otherwise. There was indeed a fall in applications from 458,800 in 1997 to 446,500 in 1998 (compared with 405,000 in 1994), but this figure has since recovered to 442,900 in 1999, with the chief executive of UCAS predicting that applications for 2001 will exceed this figure.

As might be expected (now that they are paying customers), some students are opting for the areas of study where the quickest rewards can be secured post-college: business studies and IT. More than ever before, work is dictating what shall be studied at university. *The Times* of 29 November 1999 carried a story about a Cambridge graduate with a degree in astrophysics landing a job as a Wall Street trader. Evidently the financial institutions are willing to pay top dollar for instant brains.

The interdependence of higher education and work is likely to lead to other changes in tertiary education. As organizations find that the environment in which they operate is changing, so their requirements of graduates will also change. High academic standards remain firmly on the agenda but the need for graduates with transferable skills is becoming equally important. Yet a strongly academic education does not always meet this need.

For higher education institutions, the challenge now is to maintain high academic standards while also providing students with a skill-based education. A shake-up of the reward system for academic staff will help, though alone it will be insufficient, especially as academic salaries generally are held by academics to be well out of line with what they should be.

Changes within the graduate population

Accompanying the changes in higher education policy, there has been a huge growth in the number of people entering higher education. Between 1988/89 and 1993/94, numbers are estimated to have increased by 54 per cent. This is in stark contrast to the previous five years, when growth was estimated to be 15 per cent. In total, there are now 115 universities and 68 higher education colleges catering for 1.6 million students. This represents a 100 per cent increase on figures of 25 years ago.

The most marked expansion has been at the ex-polytechnics and colleges of higher education. These account for 63 per cent of total growth. These institutions have experienced an increase of 154 per cent in the attendance rates of foreign students. The age profile of students is also changing – they are getting older. The number of mature students entering further education has increased by over 100 per cent although the latest applications figures for 2001 show a slowing down of demand. Accepting that inability to pay for the cost of studying is likely to be responsible, the Education and Employment Secretary has announced a £68 million package which includes £17 million non-repayable bursaries for mature students.

Not only is the age at entry point pushing up the average age of graduates entering the workforce, but the exit point is also being pushed back as postgraduate study increases in popularity. In the last five years, postgraduate study has almost doubled, although employment is slowing down. The overriding trend is that further and higher education are producing increasing numbers of graduates, who are, on average, older and more highly qualified than before.

In addition to changes in the size of the graduate population, the make-up of the population has changed dramatically. Although growth in general has been huge, it has not been consistent across all disciplines. In keeping with the growth of the service industry in the economy, the most significant growth in tertiary education has occurred in the areas of business, finance, IT and medicine, whereas growth in engineering, for example, has been limited.

The representation of particular groups in the graduate population is also changing. Women's representation in higher education has increased, along with that of ethnic minority students and students with disabilities. Fifty-four per cent of the applications for places in 2001 are from women. Although men have been outnumbered for some years in British higher education, this gives female applicants their biggest share to date.

The last few years have seen a proportional decline in white UK applicants. While a similar pattern has been witnessed in the black UK applicant population, UCAS figures for May 2000 show a small, but probably quite significant reversal of the trend, with applications from black applicants up 3.3 per cent for 2000–2001 courses. It is among UK applicants of Asian origin that the biggest growth has been seen: applications rose from 30,576 in 1995 (8.3 per cent of the UK applicant population) to 34,960 in 1997 (8.8 per cent) to 37,564 in 1999 or 9.7 per cent. UCAS report the rise for 2000–2001 courses to be 2.6 per cent. Although overall ethnic minority students make up only 12.4 per cent of the graduate population, this is double the ethnic minority representation in the UK population as a whole.

Applications from overseas students also rose in the '90s, although that trend has been halted. Applications from this sector are down 2.6 per cent in 2001. Ireland, where it is now much cheaper for students to stay home to take a degree, still sends by far the largest contingent of students to Britain, but numbers are down by more than 10 per cent. The drop is even larger in Greece, the biggest continental market. However, whatever happens in this sector, the graduate population in the UK has never been so diverse.

Demand for graduates

One factor which is likely to have a significant effect on the graduate recruitment market is what used to be called the 'demographic time-bomb', in particular, the notion of the ageing population. Statistics certainly support this notion. Forty per cent of the adult population in the UK is over the age of 50. It is predicted that over the next 35 years the proportion of 15- to 19-year-olds in Europe will decrease from 7 to 5 per cent. A fall of 15 million in the European Community labour force between 2000 and 2025 has also been predicted.

The overall trend is one of an increase in ageing cohorts, a decrease in younger cohorts, and a general increase in the diversity of the graduate pool. The traditional image of the graduate as a white male, aged 18–22, is out of date. In fact, this group now comprises a minority. Once the current surplus of graduates has been absorbed into the labour market, it will be those graduate recruiters who are prepared for the changes in the graduate pool who will be most able to recruit the best graduates.

Taking the graduate population overall, there are more of the following than ever before:

- graduates
- technically skilled graduates
- personally skilled graduates
- immediately capable graduates
- outstanding graduates.

It seems that graduate recruiters should be jumping for joy. The apparent surplus of able and willing graduates gives organizations the power of choice. Following the recession of the early 1990s, when graduate recruitment all but dried up, there has been a recovery in demand, quite markedly so. UCAS reports that graduate unemployment in 1999 had fallen to 5.7 per cent, down from 6.9 per cent in 1997 and the lowest during the 1990s. Seven out of ten graduates now find work immediately after completing their course and demand for graduates in certain key sectors of the economy has begun to outstrip supply, despite the increasing numbers of people going into higher education. The proportion of computer science students finding work immediately after graduating has reached 83.6 per cent, and similar record levels have been reached in accountancy (83.3 per cent) and business management (79.2 per cent).

Larger, multinational organizations are experiencing fierce competition for suitably qualified graduates, as are recruiters of IT, finance and engineering graduates. The only problem area is engineering, as it was throughout the 1990s. Graduate unemployment there was 8.3 per cent in 1999, although this was lower than in 1997.

Graduates' expectations of employers

So what is it that graduates now expect of their employers? Again, there are some emerging themes. Table 1.1 summarizes the findings of a Demos study which explored graduate expectations of employment.

Table 1.1   Graduates' expectations of employment

Current expectations	Lost expectations
Maintaining employability Variety of experience Multiple careers Autonomy 'Worthwhile work' Balanced lifestyle Comfortable lifestyle A 'graduate job'	A job for life Loyalty A linear career

It seems that today's graduates are aware that their careers will no longer remain within one organization, but rather that they will be made up of 'stepping stones' from organization to organization. The desire for flexibility and the decline of loyalty lends itself well to this type of career, where the focus is firmly on maintaining employability. However, today's graduates still expect to achieve this from the base of a 'graduate job'. What they are having to come to terms with, like everyone, is that there are no longer jobs for life and, in particular, that linear careers are a thing of the past. But, as you would expect, they have already adapted.

One of the factors which most influences a graduate's decision to apply for a job is the availability of training and development opportunities. When asked to rank eleven organizational characteristics in order of importance, graduates put training and development at number 3, after the type of work they would like, and the type of people with whom they would expect to work.

Table 1.2 outlines the perceived level of importance of the eleven characteristics. Organizations which are perceived to offer the right environment for development are now firmly on the job-hunting graduate's agenda. Even as recently as 1998, organizations would not have mentioned mentoring in their recruitment literature, but now they do. Of the 39 organizations advertising in *The Times Top 100* book (which we use as a source not because we think it is especially authoritative but because of what companies say or do not say about themselves), eight (around 20 per cent) include mentoring in their personal development tariff.

Table 1.2   Perceived importance to graduates of organizational characteristics

Characteristic	Rank order
Type of work you would like to do	1
Type of people you would like to work with	2
Training and development opportunities	3
Chances of promotion	4
Salary	5
Job security	6
Working conditions	7
Reputation/image of the organization	8
Geographical location	9
Hours expected to work	10
Benefits (company car, pension, etc.)	11

In 1994, when the study summarized in Table 1.2 was conducted, salary was ranked as the fifth most important characteristic. For today's graduates, salary is likely to become an increasingly important characteristic, constituting a need rather than a 'nice to have'. The changeover from a student grant system to one of student loans has borne down hard on many students. It has been estimated that on graduation 68 per cent of students have debts of between £3,000 and £10,000. With most students having to pay their own tuition fees, the financial burden of higher education is greater than ever before. No surprise, then, that some students should react by enrolling for those subject areas – business studies and IT – which are seen to be most bankable immediately post-college.

Another factor likely to impact on graduates' expectations of salary is the increasing number of more mature, experienced graduates with higher qualifications. As competition to recruit graduates intensifies, experienced and highly qualified graduates are more likely to realize the added value they bring to the organization in terms of their skills. This will place them in a stronger position than ever to demand bigger salaries, as they become highly marketable. The picture of the 'wet-behind-the-ears' graduate who is wholly dependent on guidance in the early part of his or her career is disappearing.

A change in the way in which society has come to view the world of work affects graduates like anyone else. Unlike the 1980s, when overriding importance was attached to work, individuals in the 1990s have been exhorted to strive for a greater balance between work and personal life. Thus the British Prime Minister's wife, Cherie Booth, writes at the end of the twentieth century: 'Respect for life outside working hours is a basic right that every employee deserves from their employer at different ages and stages in their life.'

And the desire for a balanced lifestyle crops up as one of the eight characteristics in that list of graduates' expectations (Table 1.1). Graduates can be assumed to still expect to work hard, but also want the time and space to pursue the personal interests which enable them to play hard also. Accordingly, they are likely to take a close look at an organization's values. We have noticed, however, that it is the rare employer who is prepared to get up-front with anything approximating to the sentiments expressed by Mrs Blair.

Employers' expectations

Who are the 'graduate recruiters'?

The term 'graduate recruiters' perhaps conjures up an image of large multinationals armed with glossy brochures, recruiting vast quantities of graduates and laying on structured training programmes for those they take on. These recruiters still exist, of course, but, increasingly, medium-sized and smaller organizations are absorbing the surplus of graduates and are coming to enjoy some of the benefits graduates can bring to the workplace.

What do employers expect of graduates?

That the only constant is change is a mantra we hear over and over again. Over the past ten years the structure of organizations has changed dramatically: where once they were hierarchical, they have now been largely stripped of layers of middle managers and are now much more flat in structure. With organizations also intent on pooling their resources, through mergers and acquisitions, the corporate aim is to create an organization which is lean, fit and able to succeed in a highly competitive market.

The impact on employees, and especially managers, has been dramatic. It is an everyday observation from managers that workloads have greatly increased and that to survive they have to resort to taking work home and working at weekends. The same pressures fall on newly employed graduates. Today's graduates are also required to take on far more responsibility than the graduates of ten years ago. Where graduate trainees were once cosseted with extended programmes of training, they are now expected to add value right from the start. Organizations actually talk this way: in the recruitment literature published in *The Times Top 100*, the Schlumberger organization says it seeks graduates who 'want to be challenged right from day one'. In the same publication, BNFL says it is prepared to offer 'a "real" job from day one'.

Is there still such a thing as a 'graduate job'?

Not every graduate can be a star player – given the number of graduates entering the workforce each year, that would be impossible. The parameters are shifting and the demands and roles are broadening. Indeed, graduates are increasingly used to do jobs regarded in the past as 'non-graduate jobs'. A survey conducted by the National Institute for Economic and Social Research found that, in one 12-month period, up to 45 per cent of graduates joining the finance sector were recruited into clerical jobs, for which a degree was not required.

We are seeing a changing pattern of graduate employment whereby many graduates are entering organizations directly via specific jobs, from which they are expected to make their own way. These include administrative and non-specialist/managerial roles. It has been argued that this practice has actually influenced the decrease in vacancies for traditional graduate jobs. Whether this is the case or not, it has influenced the notion of what actually constitutes a 'graduate job'.

Two tiers of graduate recruitment?

There is evidence now of a two-tier system of graduate recruitment. The upper tier constitutes those graduates who would in the past have been regarded as high flyers. The second tier consists of graduates who are viewed as valuable to the organization in terms of playing a 'second-league' role. They have been referred to as 'mid-clerical', and are those who will play a valuable part in a supportive function, whether in a specialist or an administrative role. High flyers, on the other hand, are expected to play a leading role in the organization by transforming it. These are the leaders of tomorrow. Entry to either tier is usually organized by routing graduates to 'high flyer' or 'mid-clerical' streams. Streaming might be done explicitly, at the point of entry or, implicitly, through the established graduate recruitment route for the high flyers and direct entry to specific, non-graduate jobs for graduates taking mid-clerical and administrative roles.

Six types of graduate

Two streams are one thing, but what about six? It has been suggested that there are six types of graduate:

- ■ *Fast track* – Those who are seen to be the seedcorn of the organization, who are expected to perform and in return will have the support of the organization.

- *Hit the deck running* – Those who are expected to produce high performance from day one.
- *Technical, slow-burn* – Those who are able to develop themselves and will be steady developers and workers.
- *Project employment* – Those who will be flexible and have effective team-working skills to work on new projects as the need arises.
- *Non-graduate jobs* – Those with a commercial outlook and the flexibility to work in roles as needed.
- *Part-time, short-term* – Those who are interested in using their skills in the short term only in order to fund other interests.

So, it is possible to see a diversity of roles for graduates, with fast track graduates, or high flyers, still prominent in the graduate recruitment market. In addition, however, there is a large pool of graduates of varying skill sets and interests who still have much to offer organizations. If the talents of this group are to be utilized effectively in the labour market, organizations will need to understand these different graduate profiles.

If these profiles are the *role* expectations employers have of graduates, what are the *skill* expectations? Table 1.3 outlines the key skills and attributes believed to be at a premium in the graduate market. It is clear from the table that employers' expectations of graduates have never been higher. They are now expected to bring a mixture of academic, technical and personal skills to their employer. From this base they are expected to add value from day one and be adaptable to changing circumstances,

Table 1.3   What attributes employers expect graduates to arrive with

Employer 1	Employer 2	Employer 3	Employer 4	Employer 5
Specialist/ technical skills	Achievers with task flexibility	Commercial awareness	Technical skills	Teamworking
Self-reliant	Commitment to organization and role	Leadership skills	Personal skills	Interpersonal skills
Teamworking	Good learning skills	Interpersonal skills	Immediately capable	Communication skills
Business skills and knowledge	Providing minimal risk and high return		Outstanding skills	

whether this be the task they are expected to achieve or the people with whom they are expected to work. Those graduates who are unable to meet these expectations can still have a valuable part to play in organizations in one of the alternative roles springing up outside the traditional graduate position.

The costs of graduate recruitment

Graduate recruitment is a costly affair. The median starting salary for a graduate in 1996 was reckoned to be £14,750, an increase of 5.3 per cent on the previous year. By 1999 many of the larger graduate recruiters were offering starting salaries closer to £30,000. Andersen Consulting paid starting salaries of £25,000, with a £1,750 signing-on bonus, while some finance houses offered £30,000 plus with bonuses of up to £5,000. The highest starting salary was £42,000. The most recent survey (by Incomes Data Services) reported that the median starting salary for graduates was expected to rise to £18,000 in 2000 from £17,500 in 1999. Almost a quarter of employers said they paid 'golden hellos', or special bonuses, to recruits.

Recruitment costs have risen, too. In 1996 these were estimated at £4,600 per graduate: by 2000, the figure was not far short of £6000. Although the milk-round has been seen in the past to be a cost-effective way of managing recruitment, this is changing. Careers services, which traditionally organized recruiter visits for free, are beginning to charge back the costs of this service. In addition, more and more organizations are requiring graduates to apply through often specially dedicated websites, but they have not given up the milk-round just yet.

Then there are the time and resources necessary to conduct effective graduate recruitment. Top-of-the-line techniques such as assessment centres are now commonplace, but they are still time-consuming and expensive to run. And preceding attendance at an assessment centre are all the costs of processing, screening, interviewing, short-listing, and so on.

Graduate recruiters are not exempt from the demand for added value. Traditional methods of recruiting graduates are history, and recruiters now have to box clever. Just recruiting graduates is not enough: the hard bit is retaining them. We have more to say on this in Chapter 10.

Key points from this chapter

■ The last ten years has seen the context of graduate recruitment change fundamentally, and forever.
■ The boom in further and higher education is producing increasing numbers of graduates, who are, on average, older and more highly

qualified than before. There are in the UK now 1.6 million students, a 100 per cent increase on 25 years ago.

- More than ever before, work is dictating what shall be studied at university. With loans to pay off, students are opting for the most bankable studies.
- High academic standards remain firmly on the agenda but the need for graduates with transferable skills is becoming just as important.
- Women's representation in higher education has increased, along with that of ethnic minority students and students with disabilities.
- The trend for applications from black applicants showed a small upward reversal for 2000–2001 courses, while the biggest growth has been seen among home applicants of Asian origin.
- Seven out of ten graduates now find work immediately after completing their course; demand for graduates in certain key sectors of the economy has begun to outstrip supply, despite the increasing numbers going into higher education.
- The three strongest factors affecting graduates' decisions to apply for a job are (in order) the type of work they would like, the type of people with whom they would expect to work, and the availability of training and development opportunities.
- Beyond the high flyers there is a large pool of graduates of varying skill sets and interests who have much to offer. Organizations will need to understand this pool if they are to utilize it effectively.
- Graduate recruitment is an expensive affair: opening salaries are up and the costs of recruitment have never been higher.
- Just recruiting graduates is not enough: the hard bit is retaining them.

Sending the right message

Organizations complain that they cannot attract the quality of applicants they require or would like. However, they may not always understand that the message they send and the way it is interpreted by possible applicants is a critical factor in determining whether a recruitment drive is going to be successful.

It's important to distinguish between the *corporate image* and the *recruitment message*. The corporate image is what the organization would like you to admire most about it. Usually, this image trades on a considerable history of image fixing in the public imagination. Is there – will there ever be – a greater image than Rolls-Royce? Not only is it associated in everyone's mind with excellence and superiority, it can even be loaned out, as it were, to give other processes the Rolls-Royce stamp of quality.

The recruitment message is less glamorous and more elusive. It is about what the organization is looking for and how it will treat recruits, as reflected in its hiring practices. Evidently, it is much more difficult to get over a distinctive recruitment message; on the other hand, it is where the professionalism of graduate recruiters really comes to the fore.

Riding on the corporate image

The information that graduates bring to bear on initial application decisions is based largely on general impressions of organizational attractiveness. If they warm to (Sir) Richard Branson and his disdain for the stuffy and the unadventurous, and like his tie-less, laid-back action man image, then they will probably be attracted to Virgin. If they find the idea of flying round the world glamorous, and buy into the slogan of BA as the world's favourite airline, then they might apply to British Airways (whether they get to fly round the world is another matter). If they like the way Tesco rolled up its sleeves and saw off Sainsburys, and now wants to do the same to WalMart, or if they just like Tesco's bustling, mercantile image, then you might apply to them. In its heyday, Marks & Spencer was at the top of the graduate tree, presumably due to its widely known success. Now that the company has been taking knocks, it will be interesting to see if it continues to have the same appeal for graduates.

These associations suggest immediately that organizations could improve their attractiveness to applicants by identifying the key elements of their image and then modifying or improving the message they portray to the target audience. No graduate would have wanted to apply to Tesco in their 'Pile it high, sell 'em cheap days' (which were not so long ago), but look at them now.

What sort of corporate image does the Civil Service – the top echelons, that is – possess? Snooty, peopled by Oxbridge mandarins, exclusive, rejecting – is this the image still? Judging by the title of a 1999 advertisement and the implication that most people simply wouldn't be good enough – 'You aren't working for us, but could you?' – the answer would seem to be affirmative.

At least the Civil Service has a corporate image, even if it does not always work in its favour. Most organizations simply do not have a corporate image, unless it be anonymously dull.

Formulating the recruitment message

The recruitment message is what you tell graduates you are looking for. Usually, and increasingly, the message is formulated in terms of skills, qualifications and abilities, but not always. An organization might offer nothing further than 'growth, vision and strength', with mentor provided (for example, British Steel in *The Times Top 100*). Goodness knows what a graduate would make of that. The sell must be on the corporate image (in British Steel's case, old public sector failed monster turned around by private sector drive and enterprise).

Do all organizations come up with a recruitment message? By no means. Some do not bother at all. British Airways (amazingly considering all the work done for it on competencies and values) confines itself in its *Times Top 100* entry to talk of graduates bringing new skills and perspectives, with mentors and buddies thrown in. Unless this is loose language, it is intriguing to speculate on what those new skills and perspectives could be. To our knowledge, no one else has ever suggested that graduates actually generate new skills.

Marks & Spencer are the same as BA, judging from their entry in *The Times Top 100*. They transmit no recruitment message as such, just 'the opportunity to put all that theory into practice'. Maybe they feel they don't need to try, that the corporate image will do it all for them. And they might be right. Companies without a distinctive corporate image have to work that much harder to attract the best talent.

If you want to attract suitable applicants, then they should be able to differentiate between you and other organizations. The capacity of an organization to attract the applicants it requires depends to a large degree on its success in making known the opportunities it has to offer.

Many of the key messages that organizations are trying to project are either lost or understated amidst the bundles of glossy brochures, pamphlets and application forms that graduates accumulate. We found that many possible applicants were unaware of the key criteria that employers apply when evaluating graduate applicants. Students may think that it is their qualifications and previous work experience which matter but employers look also (and sometimes mainly) for their personal qualities and skills. Table 2.1 makes the point.

Table 2.1   Criteria looked for in potential applicants according to employers and students

Criteria that employers were looking for in potential applicants	Rank Order	Rank Order	Student's perceptions of criteria that employers were looking for in potential applicants
Personal qualities	1	1	Specific graduate qualification
Specific skills	2	2	Previous related work experience
Specific graduate qualification	3	3	Personal qualities
Previous related work experience	4	4	Specific skills
Previous unrelated work experience	5	5	Previous unrelated work experience

Two kinds of recruitment message

Whether they are doing it implicitly or explicitly, consciously or unconsciously, organizations basically use two kinds of recruitment message: a competency-based message, and a values-based message.

Competency-based messages

Competencies emerge from a job analysis of the graduate role. Competency-based recruitment messages describe outcomes expected from the performance of professional functions, or knowledge, skills and attitudes thought to be essential to the performance in those functions. ICL, for example, stated in 1997: 'In addition to professional knowledge specific to their roles in the Company, our people need to be intelligent and adaptable with the initiative and tenacity to meet and exceed our customer's requirements and take our business forward.' For their part, Coopers & Lybrand (as it was) preferred to say: 'The people who join us today will contribute to our future success. Entrepreneurs, creative and inventive individuals; all will shape our future business. Our people need to have strong analytical minds, be able to measure risk, be decisive in tough situations and be clear thinking in a business environment of constant change.'

Deconstructing these two statements, it can be seen that competencies are expressed in terms of:

- personal characteristics (e.g. tenacity)
- skills and knowledge (e.g. analytical skills)
- attitude and orientation (e.g. contribution to future success)
- job-required outputs and skills (e.g. measurement risk, decisiveness, taking the business forward).

Evidently, talking in terms of competencies has clear advantages:

- It helps organizations achieve a closer match between a person's skills and interests and the demands of the job.
- It improves accuracy in identifying the appropriate criteria for the role and provide a clear framework for recruitment.
- It helps organizations sharpen their message by eliminating that which is irrelevant to the position.
- It provides a language to help organizations communicate their needs.
- It facilitates criterion-referenced assessment.

These are solid advantages, but there is a problem. What if, instead of helping potential applicants to differentiate between organizations, using competency language only succeeds in highlighting the similarities? Here is how a company with no corporate image whatsoever, operating in a specialist market, projects its recruitment message:

ARE YOU?

- Confident, dynamic, ambitious?
- A strong communicator?
- Flexible, adaptable, eager to learn?
- A self-starter with the ability to work on own initiative?
- A good team player?

Could anything possibly be missing from this wish list? It seems that only gods need apply! Seriously, though, how could any other organization, large or small, differentiate from that idealized conception of a graduate?

Compare the above with a much plainer advertisement from a public body:

> The Council is seeking administrators with a degree or equivalent for two key departments – Fitness to Practise and Education.
>
> Good communications, organisational and analytical skills, self-motivation and PC literacy are required for each post.

It too is couched in competency language but the absence of hyperbole ('strong', 'eager', 'dynamic') actually clears the way for the potential applicant, if he or she is honest, to say simply 'yes' or 'no' to each of the five competencies and then score the result. Four out of five you might apply, three probably not.

Table 2.2 shows the key recruitment criteria for four different organizations as outlined in their recruitment brochures.

Table 2.2   Examples of competency-based recruitment messages

Coopers & Lybrand	Civil Service – fast stream	ICL	British Airways
Drive and initiative	Achievement orientated Initiative	Initiates action Organizes time to achieve objectives	Action orientation Learning orientation Calculated risk-taking
Interpersonal skills	Interpersonal skills Communication skills	Influences people Works with others to achieve goals	Leadership Teamworking Communication
Problem-solving	Practical problem-solving ability	Identifies problems and solutions quickly	Problem analysis
Commitment to a business career		Understands what 'business' means	

Would a graduate – or anyone – really be able to distinguish between these organizations? Perhaps the language is too familiar, and too much is taken for granted. Of course, graduates assume, that is what employers require. However, what is *actually* required is greater integration between the projection of the competencies required and the organizational image.

Values-based messages

Values-based recruitment rests on the core principles of the organization, what it stands for and believes in. Unlike competency statements, value statements encourage potential applicants to focus on whether they can *identify with* an organization, as opposed to *meeting* its recruitment criteria. Evidently, values can be used to attract the applicant you want and, in a kind of realistic job preview (see Chapter 5), values can be used to put off the applicants you do not want. The following examples give the general idea.

The case of Innovex: attracting the applicants you want

A company called Innovex wished to recruit part-time and term-time pharmaceutical representatives. It needed to find people who wanted to combine a successful selling job with their other commitments. Their recruitment advertisement portrayed three childlike drawings of women, one ironing, one with a mobile phone, and one with two bags of shopping.

The caption underneath read 'Whose mum works for Innovex?' Although they homed in on women in their advertisement, they made it clear that the work could be suitable for mothers, fathers, or anyone who wanted a part-time job. The Innovex recruitment message was successful because it outlined clearly that this job was only part-time, and was not a way into a future, more permanent, post. Furthermore, the organization clearly understood and respected that people had priorities/commitments in life other than work.

Price Waterhouse: putting off the applicants you do not want

When it was still Price Waterhouse, PricewaterhouseCooper once ran a recruitment campaign for consultants which featured six recruitment advertisements all headed: 'Reasons not to join Price Waterhouse as a management consultant'. The caption for change-management consultants read 'I like telling people what to do', while the caption for IT consultants for the financial sector read 'I just want to make a quick killing'.

These messages emphasize behaviours and motives that did not reflect the values of Price Waterhouse. They make it clear that, if you fitted the description, then Price Waterhouse was not for you.

Core values say an awful lot about an organization – perhaps they tell you all you need to know. Consider these examples:

- *Walt Disney:*
    - no cynicism
    - nurturing and promulgation of 'wholesome American values'
    - creativity, dreams and imagination
    - fanatical attention to consistency and detail
    - preservation and control of the Disney magic.

- *Philip Morris:*
    - the right to freedom of choice
    - winning, beating others in a good fight

- encouraging individual initiative
- opportunity based on merit; no one is entitled to anything
- hard work and continuous self-improvement.

■ *Sony:*
- elevation of the Japanese culture and national status
- being a pioneer, not following others; doing the impossible
- encouraging individual ability and creativity.

■ *Nordstrom:*
- service to the customer above all else
- hard work and individual productivity
- never being satisfied
- excellence in reputation; being part of something special.

These short simple statements give more of a flavour of what it would be like to work in these companies than any number of 'personal testimonies' or case studies. The most impressive thing about them is their honesty – they certainly would not appeal to all. For example, we doubt whether the person who is attracted to apply to Philip Morris ('winning', 'beating others in a good fight') would also be tempted to apply to Walt Disney ('no cynicism', 'nurturing and promulgation of "wholesome American values"').

One of the key challenges for recruiters is to persuade applicants to put the effort into differentiating between employers and between positions, and to target their applications. From the applicant's point of view it may make sense to use the scattergun approach; they will think that the more applications they send the greater the likelihood of getting an interview, and ultimately a job. That said, persuading people, in the nicest possible way, to think about who they are applying to, and why, must surely make the recruitment process more efficient for both parties.

Integrating the messages

Have you got what we want? Do you want to work with us? These are the questions an applicant needs to ponder. On its own, competency-based recruitment will not do. If the reason for improving the recruitment message is to improve the fit between the applicant and the organization, then it surely makes sense that the values of the organization should be integrated into this message from the beginning.

How graduates perceive employers

We have been examining the message an organization sends out. Now we need to look at how messages are interpreted by potential applicants.

To discover how graduates perceive employers and the factors which influence their decisions to apply for a job, we ran a series of three surveys focusing on: graduates' perceptions of employers, ethnic minority graduates' perceptions of employers, and graduate's perceptions of employers' recruitment and selection practices. The surveys were primarily questionnaire-based and supported by interviews. The findings incorporate the responses of over 800 students from universities all over England.

The research covered three key areas:

■ the organizations that students are most and least likely to apply to
■ the organizational characteristics that students find attractive
■ the sources of job information that students are most likely to use.

The organizations that students are most and least likely to apply to

Students rated the attractiveness of each of 54 well-known organizations. These did not include the management consultancies like Andersens or the City finance houses. The top ten organizations that students are most likely to apply to are shown in Table 2.3.

Table 2.3   Top organizations for all students

Characteristic	Respondents %	Rank order
British Airways	29.0	1
BBC	27.0	2
Virgin Airlines	25.0	3
Boots	22.0	4
British Petroleum	21.0	5
British Telecom	20.0	6
Marks & Spencer	19.8	7
Cadbury Schweppes	19.0	8
LWT	18.5	9
Smith Kline Beecham	18.5	9
Shell	18.5	9

According to these data, where choice was from a pre-formed list, British Airways (29 per cent) was the organization that students would be most likely to apply to. The BBC (27 per cent) and Virgin Airlines (25 per cent) were second and third choice. These three organizations were consistently identified within the top five organizations for each of the different student groups.

The top ten list contains no public sector organizations, suggesting that high-profile, private sector organizations are considered by our student sample to be a more attractive option for graduate-level jobs.

Table 2.4 shows ten organizations that students are *least* likely to apply. Over three-quarters of the respondents (77 per cent) reported that the Army was the organization that they were least likely to apply to. Eight of the ten organizations that all students were least likely to apply to were public sector organizations. The uniformed forces dominate this list: the Army, the Derbyshire Police, the Royal Air Force, the Royal Navy and the Metropolitan Police.

Table 2.4   Ten organizations that students were least likely to apply to

Organization	Respondents %	Rank order
Army	77.0	1
Derbyshire Police	73.0	2
Royal Air Force	70.0	3
Royal Navy	70.0	4
London Underground	70.0	5
Railtrack	67.0	6
Metropolitan Police	67.0	6
Coventry City Council	65.0	8
Birmingham City Council	62.0	9
Department of Transport	58.0	10

It would appear that while students have little specific knowledge about organizations as graduate recruiters, they are generally more aware of private sector recruiters than of those in the public sector. Even with very little knowledge, students can still clearly separate out those organizations which they consider to be more attractive, i.e. those with a higher public profile. This implies that the decision to apply to an organization for a graduate job is more likely to be based on a general image of that organization than on specific knowledge. Glamour and sexiness seem to be the driving factors.

The implications for managing the recruitment process are quite far-reaching:

■ Public sector organizations will have smaller applicant pools and are likely to have more difficulty attracting the diversity of candidates necessary for successful selection decisions.
■ Private sector organizations are likely to attract large numbers of

inappropriate candidates, as well as appropriate ones, making the selection task more problematic.

■ The corporate image projected by an organization – its glamour, if you like – is more likely than its recruitment message to trigger graduate application decisions.

The organizational characteristics that students find attractive

Students were asked to indicate the relevance of each of 36 organizational characteristics in their decision to apply to an organization for employment. The top ten characteristics for all students are reported in Table 2.5.

Table 2.5   Top ten organizational characteristics for all students

Characteristic	Respondents %	Rank order
Stimulating	60.0	1
Equal opportunities employer	53.0	2
Professional	51.0	3
Friendly	48.0	4
Fair	47.0	5
Respectful	46.0	6
Enthusiastic	36.0	7
Financially secure	35.0	8
Fun	34.5	9
Safe	34.0	10

The majority of students (60 per cent) rated 'stimulating' as an essential characteristic of a future employer. Other characteristics such as 'professional', 'friendly', and 'fair', were also consistently ranked within the top ten in all student groups. Only three – 'stimulating', 'equal opportunities employer' and 'professional' – were considered to be essential by over 50 per cent of the sample.

The top five most *off-putting* organizational characteristics for all students were:

■ cut-throat (53%)
■ risky (32%)
■ profit-driven (17%)

- small (17%)
- community-based (10%).

Two key points emerge from this research. First, it is clear that many of the more attractive organizational characteristics can be picked up either from an organization's recruitment message or from its corporate image. Second, it appears likely that it is the corporate image which is most likely to deter students from applying.

An interpretation of this for graduate recruiters is that, whilst both the recruitment message and corporate image will attract graduate applicants, the corporate image is more likely to be the one that can negatively influence potentially suitable applicants.

Sources of information and advertising that students are likely to use

It emerges that there is a strong similarity between the sources that employers use to advertise their graduate vacancies and those that students use when looking for job information – see Table 2.6.

Table 2.6   Where employers advertise and where students look for information

Employers	Students
Career library folders (56%)	Career-library folders (79%)
Graduate recruitment fairs (45%)	Graduate recruitment fairs (71%)
Graduate Employment and Training (GET) (41%)	Graduate Opportunities (GO) (67%)
Graduate Opportunities (GO) (34%)	Graduate Employment and Training (GET) (63%)
Regional papers/ Milk-round (33%)	Regional/local papers (60%)

Four of the top five sources that organizations use for advertising graduates are centred around the university careers offices, that is, careers library folders, GET, GO, and the milk-round. Some differences emerged between the advertising strategies used by organizations in the public and private sectors, for example:

- Private sector organizations (63 per cent) ranked career library folders as their most popular source of graduate recruitment advertising. However, career library folders were ranked as third choice for the public sector organizations (37 per cent).

- Newspapers and the media are more frequently used by public sector organizations to advertise their graduate recruitment than by the private sector. Both regional/local newspapers (50 per cent) and the *Guardian* (33 per cent) were in the top five for the public sector.

As Table 2.6 shows, most students are likely to use career library folders as part of their job information-seeking strategy. It follows that students are likely to gain more information about private sector than public sector organizations, and indeed students seem to be more aware of organizations in the private than the public sector.

Competition for graduates is intensifying as never before. If they are to compete, organizations must focus clearly not only upon the image they want to project, but also upon the image they already have. And they must find ways to send out unequivocal messages, in unusual language perhaps or through unusual modalities if need be (for example, Asda once advertised in *Viz* with great success), in order to communicate to graduates what they are looking for and what they have to offer.

Key points from this chapter

- The message an organization sends out and the way it is interpreted by possible applicants is a critical factor in determining whether a recruitment drive is going to be successful.
- There is a distinction between the *corporate image* and the *recruitment message*. The corporate image is what the organization would like you to admire most about it. The less glamorous and moe elusive recruitment message is about what the organization is looking for and how it will treat you, as reflected in the way it will try to hire you.
- The recruitment message has two elements: the competencies sought in applicants, and the values the applicant can expect the organization to enact.
- Unlike competency statements, value statements encourage potential applicants to focus on whether they can *identify with* an organization, as opposed to *meeting* its recruitment criteria.
- The capacity of an organization to attract the applicants it requires depends to a large degree on its enterprise in making known the opportunities it has to offer.
- A key challenge for recruiters is to persuade applicants to put the effort into differentiating between employers and between positions, and to target their applications.
- Graduates themselves regard high-profile, private sector organizations as a more attractive option than the public sector.
- It is the corporate image which is most likely to deter students from applying.

■ In order to communicate successfully to graduates what they are looking for and what they have to offer, organizations must face the challenge of finding ways to send out distinctive (but not gimmicky) messages, maybe using unusual language and/or media.

The current practice of graduate recruitment, and what graduates think of it

To gain insights into current practices of graduate recruitment and selection in organizations, and how these are perceived by graduates, we undertook two surveys: one of graduate recruiting organizations throughout the UK, the other of final-year undergraduates who were applying for graduate jobs. From this research, therefore, we are able not only to describe the processes that organizations are currently using to recruit and select graduates but also what the people who are on the receiving end, i.e. the graduates, think of them. This work provides unique insights into how selection processes can affect the perceptions of an organization by potential employees.

A total of 109 organizations replied to our survey, 71 per cent from the private sector, and 29 per cent from the public sector. The top four industrial sectors from which we received responses were the government (29 per cent), consumer goods and manufacturing (23 per cent), banking and finance (18 per cent), and consultancy and professional (14 per cent). Follow-up interviews with ten personnel managers and specialists in graduate recruitment were also conducted.

For our survey of graduates a questionnaire was distributed at various universities throughout England. A total of 442 replies were received. Fifty-three per cent were male, 44 per cent were female, and 3 per cent did not specify their gender. Ethnic minority students made up 18 per cent of the sample. Nine students mentioned a disability.

Overview of graduate recruitment

Organizations were asked about the frequency of their graduate recruitment schemes. We also examined the number of graduate applications they received each year, and the percentage of those applicants who received job offers.

Frequency of graduate recruitment

Table 3.1 indicates that 56 per cent of organizations in the private sector run a graduate recruitment scheme once a year compared to 32 per cent of the public sector organizations. In addition, the majority of organizations in the sectors of consultancy and professional (57 per cent), banking and finance (61 per cent), and consumer goods and manufacturing (56 per cent) run a graduate recruitment scheme once a year.

Table 3.1 How often employers run their graduate recruitment scheme

Frequency	Public sector organizations (%)	Private sector organizations (%)
Once a year	32	56
More than once a year	25	26
Less than once a year	43	18

Number of graduate applications received per year

Table 3.2 shows the number of graduate applications received per year. Almost half the organizations in both the public and private sector receive over 750 graduate applications each year. For high-profile organizations the number of graduate applications is more likely to be in the region of 2000 to 4000.

Table 3.2 Number of graduate applications received by public and private sector organizations

Number of graduate applications per year	Public sector organizations (%)	Private sector organizations (%)
Up to 250	22	36
251–750	32	19
More than 750	46	45

Percentage of applicants who receive job offers

As Table 3.3 shows, 72 per cent of organizations in the sample offered jobs to 5 per cent or less of initial graduate applicants. Over one-third (36 per cent) of the public sector organizations offered positions to 11 per cent or more of initial applicants. Only one-tenth of the private sector organizations in our sample offered this number of positions.

Table 3.3   Percentage of graduate applicants who receive job offers

Per cent	All organizations (%)	Public sector (%)	Private sector (%)
Up to 5	72	59	75
6–10	11	5	15
11–20	10	27	4
More than 20	6.5	9	6

Public sector organizations conduct graduate recruitment schemes less frequently than private sector organizations and they receive fewer job applications. The public sector would appear to be less attractive as an employer than the private sector.

Recruitment processes that organizations are using

Organizations use both application and assessment processes when recruiting graduates.

The application process

As Table 3.4 shows, the majority of organizations (54 per cent) short-listed for graduate positions using an application form only. This was true for both public and private sectors.

Table 3.4   Application processes used for graduate recruitment and selection

	All organizations (%)	Private sector (%)	Public sector (%)
Application form only	54	49	69
CV required only	14	16	10
Application form and CV	21	27	7
Applications on Internet	20	24	11
Reference letters	92	88	97

It is worth noting that 20 per cent of organizations accept applications via the Internet, although this mode is more popular in the private sector (24 per cent) than in the public sector (11 per cent). Interestingly, 33 per cent of the private sector organizations, and 27 per cent of the public sector organizations, now advertise their graduate vacancies on the Net. We found that many organizations are advertising on the Internet because it is 'the thing to do' and because they 'had to keep up with the market'. Technological limitations were seen as the main reason why organizations had not developed Internet facilities to accept applications. However, many organizations felt that the Internet was an area where further developments would continue to occur, mainly due to the growth in international recruitment, the need to target students outside the UK, and the need to maintain a competitive edge.

Almost all employers (92 per cent) stated that they collect reference letters at some stage of the application process. In the majority of cases (77 per cent), references did not form part of the selection criteria, but were collected as a final check *after* a conditional offer had been made.

How students apply
By far the most common method students use to apply to an organization is an application form (Table 3.5). This is to be expected given that the majority of organizations use nothing more than an application form for shortlisting.

Table 3.5   Information asked for during the application process

	All respondents (%)	White students (%)	Ethnic minority students (%)
Application form	95	96	98
Curriculum vitae	85	87	93
Covering letter	77	80	84
Biodata	17	18	31
CV via e-mail	9	6	25
CV via the Internet	7	6	18

There are differences here between white and ethnic minority students' experiences. First, almost twice as many ethnic minority students (31 per cent) as white students (17 per cent) completed biodata as part of their application process. Second, the percentage of ethnic minority students who had sent applications via e-mail and the Internet was much greater than the percentage of white students.

These results raise intriguing questions. Are ethnic minority students more likely than white students to use the Internet when looking for a job? If so, does this reflect the type of jobs that they are looking for? Is the Net – or biodata come to that, being more impersonal – seen as a safer, that is, more neutral medium for applying?

The assessment process

Organizations were asked about their assessment processes and the methods of assessment they use when selecting graduates.

Assessment process and types of assessment methods used
An assessment process usually comprises a series of stages. Two stages of assessment were most commonly used within both the public and the private sector. However, some subtle differences emerged:

■ 80 per cent of organizations in the private sector have two stages of assessment after shortlisting, 11 per cent have three, and 9 per cent have one.
■ 50 per cent of organizations in the public sector have two stages of assessment after shortlisting, 25 per cent have three, and 35 per cent have one.

Sixty per cent of both public and private sector organizations in our sample used assessment centres (see Table 3.6). Of these:

- 79 per cent used structured interviews
- 79 per cent used group discussions
- 65 per cent used presentations
- 64 per cent used ability tests
- 51 per cent used case study exercises
- 49 per cent used personality questionnaires
- 49 per cent used work sample tests
- 32 per cent used role-play exercises
- 11 per cent used unstructured interviews.

Regarding assessment centres, there were some differences between public and private sector organizations with respect to their top five most commonly used assessment methods, as Table 3.6 shows.

Table 3.6 Top five assessment methods used in graduate assessment centres

Public sector	Organizations (%)	Private sector	Organizations (%)
1. Group discussion	81	1. Structured interviews	80
2. Structured interviews	75	2. Group discussion	78
3. Work samples/case studies/ability tests	62	3. Presentation	67
4. Presentation	56	4. Ability tests	65
5. Personality questionnaire	44	5. Personality questionnaire	49

The most frequently used exercises, for both public and private sector, were structured interviews and group discussions. Role-plays and unstructured interviews were the two least used methods of assessment.

Work sample tests and case study exercises were used more frequently as part of the assessment centre process by the public sector. However, presentations were more likely to be used by the private sector.

Equal opportunities and assessor training

The research came up with some interesting findings with regard to equal opportunity monitoring, and the training given to assessors/selectors.

Equal opportunity monitoring in graduate recruitment

Organizations were asked whether they conducted any form of equal opportunity (EO) monitoring within their graduate recruitment process. Table 3.7 shows the results.

Table 3.7   Frequency of equal opportunity monitoring in graduate recruitment schemes

	All organizations	Public sector (%)	Private sector (%)
Conducts EO monitoring	61	73	56
Does not conduct EO monitoring	39	27	44

It is a matter of some concern to find that well over a third of the organizations in our sample did not conduct *any* equal opportunity monitoring. Of those organizations that did, monitoring was more prevalent amongst public sector organizations.

Some private sector organizations that did collect equal opportunity data admitted – when they were candid – that they were not monitoring the results closely or making any use of the data whatsoever. Interviews within the public sector, however, revealed a different emphasis on equal opportunities. For example, one recruiter commented: 'Our intake of ethnic minorities at present is too low – we won't be comfortable until it reflects the balance in society generally.'

These results are somewhat surprising given the increasing emphasis on equal opportunities in the workplace. The major benefit of conducting equal opportunity monitoring is that it helps organizations to identify any practice or procedure which may impact unfairly on a particular applicant group; this, incidentally, reduces the chances of provoking an industrial tribunal.

Yet so many organizations do not collect or make use of monitoring data. Or they do collect (because they have been told that is the right thing to do) and then do not make use of the received data. A coherent approach is therefore required, where all equal opportunity data are collected and regularly monitored.

It is also clear that the public sector must do more to inform candidates on what it has to offer. Significantly, the supposed commitment to equal opportunities is not being picked up by ethnic minority students. If it were, the public sector might find the number of ethnic minorities it employs increasing.

There is scope for organizations to adopt a more systematic and beneficial approach to equal opportunity monitoring. Presently almost 40 per cent of organizations do not conduct any form of monitoring whatsoever. We found that monitoring, where it did take place, was more prevalent amongst public sector organizations although there is still a way to go.

The training organizations give to assessors

Organizations were asked about the amount of training they gave to individuals involved in screening, interviewing and assessing graduates. Table 3.8 lists the results.

Table 3.8   The amount of training given to assessors/selectors

	3 or more days %		1-2 days %		Less than 1 day %		None %	
	Public	Private	Public	Private	Public	Private	Public	Private
Screening application forms/CV	22	10	44	31	22	24	12	35
Interview skills training	25	19	71	66	4	10	0	6
Assessor training for assessment centres	56	20	19	51	25	20	0	9
Training to use ability tests or personality questionnaires	67	60	17	13	6	6	10	21

An alarming finding to emerge from these results is the lack of training being given to assessors at the screening and selection stages, specifically:

- 35 per cent of private sector organizations in the sample gave no training to individuals in the screening of application forms/CVs as opposed to 12 per cent of public sector organizations.
- 6 per cent of private sector organizations gave no interview skills training to assessors.
- In the public sector the most common time-span for assessor training was three or more days (56 per cent). This is in contrast to the most common duration in the private sector, which was one to two days (51 per cent).
- 9 per cent of private sector organizations that use assessment centres gave no training for assessors whatsoever.

In addition, our findings show that 60 per cent of private sector and 67 per cent of public sector organizations gave three or more days' training in the use of ability tests and personality questionnaires. These figures are quite high in comparison to the training given for other assessment methods, which may be due to the fact that these courses are usually run externally and for those stipulated periods. However, what is most concerning is that 21 per cent of private sector organizations, and 10 per cent of public sector organizations, actually use these tests/questionnaires with untrained personnel!

There appears to be a lack of training being given to assessors at the screening and selection stages. In our experience, untrained assessors are less likely to make objective, consistent and fair decisions within the selection process. This will have a significant bearing on the fairness of the system and on the quality of the graduates being assessed.

What graduates say about their assessment experiences

We asked graduates to rate the assessment methods they perceived to be the most fair and relevant, and those which they perceived to be the least – the results can be seen in Table 3.9.

Table 3.9   The most relevant and fair assessment methods (as perceived by graduates)

Most relevant methods	Respondents (%)	Fairest methods	Respondents (%)
1. Interviews	59	1. Interviews	81
2. Work sample test	25	2. Work sample test	54
3. Ability tests	21	3. Ability tests	54

The three most relevant and fairest assessment methods, as perceived by students, are interviews, work samples, and ability tests. We asked some graduates about the reasons behind their perceptions. Some of their responses were:

- 'Interviews are fair because they are a two-way evaluation process between the employer and the interviewee.'
- 'Interviews give you an opportunity to sell yourself.'
- 'Work samples give real life experience of the job.'
- 'With work samples, you can see if you are cut out for the job, and if you would enjoy it.'
- 'Ability tests give an indication of individuals' strengths and weaknesses, and they are vital for some occupations.'

What did graduates think were the *least fair* and *least relevant* assessment methods? Table 3.10 shows that graduates perceived role-plays and personality questionnaires as the least relevant and most unfair assessment methods. Case studies (least relevant) and group discussions (unfair) were also disliked.

Table 3.10   The least relevant and fair assessment methods (as perceived by graduates)

Least relevant methods	Respondents (%)	Most unfair methods	Respondents (%)
1. Role-play	41	1. Role-play	37
2. Personality questionnaires	28	2. Personality questionnaires	35
3. Case study	26	3. Group discussion	26

Reasons for students' perceptions of these methods included:

- 'Role-plays are unfair – I did not apply to be an actor.'
- 'Role-plays are unrealistic and alien to how you would behave.'
- 'Personality questionnaires are not related to your ability to do the job.'
- 'One can always bluff personality questionnaires in order to suit the employers' needs.'
- 'Case studies are not always very realistic, and they can be too intense.'
- 'Case studies can be biased towards business knowledge.'

Obviously, there is some unease about certain selection methods and their perceived fairness. Understandably, graduates want to learn more about what a job would entail and whether they are cut out for it, so they like any assessment method which assists in that. Assessment methods which allow two-way communication and evaluation are found to be relevant and fair.

These findings are important. We know that word of mouth matters, and it would be reasonable to assume that what graduates hear from others about an organization's assessment process may affect whether they apply to that organization or, indeed, accept an offer should one be made.

Key points from this chapter

■ Public sector organizations tend to run graduate recruitment schemes less frequently than private sector organizations, and receive fewer unsolicited job applications. The public sector would appear to be less attractive as an employer than the private sector.

■ The most common method students use to apply to an organization is an application form – the majority of organizations use nothing more than an application form for shortlisting.

■ Recruitment via the Internet is increasing rapidly, mainly due to the growth in international recruitment, the need to target students outside the UK, and the need to maintain a competitive edge.

■ Ethnic minority students are much more inclined than their white counterparts to send applications via e-mail and the Internet; perhaps the Net – and biodata – are seen as a safer, more neutral, application medium.

■ Where assessment centres are used, the most frequently used exercises, for both public and private sector, are structured interviews and group discussions. Role-plays and unstructured interviews are the least used assessment methods.

■ Well over a third of the organizations in our sample did not conduct any equal opportunity monitoring, which was more prevalent in the public sector.

■ The public sector must do more to inform candidates on what it has to offer. Significantly, the supposed commitment to equal opportunities is not being picked up by ethnic minority students. If it were, the public sector might find an increase in the number of ethnic minorities' employees.

■ Assessors need more training on how to screen and select, as untrained assessors are less likely than trained assessors to make objective, consistent and fair decisions.

■ The three most relevant and fairest assessment methods, as students perceive them, are interviews, work samples and ability tests. The least are role-plays and personality questionnaires. Case studies and group discussions are also disliked.

- Graduates like any assessment method which helps them learn more about what a job would entail and whether they are cut out for it, especially methods which permit two-way communication and evaluation.
- Word of mouth matters. What graduates hear about an organization's assessment process may affect whether they apply to that organization or, indeed, accept an offer should one be made.

'But they just don't apply': what ethnic minority graduates want

The proportion of ethnic minority graduates is increasing, and in the future they will represent a significantly larger percentage of the labour supply. Yet many organizations report that ethnic minorities do not apply to them in the same proportions as white graduates. This chapter takes up this issue and explains why a lack of applicants from this sector of the graduate population should be a worry for employers.

We describe the findings from our research on ethnic minority graduate perceptions of employers. We focus in particular on unpacking the concept of organizational image and how it may be perceived differently by different ethnic groups, trying to surface those factors which may be influencing applications from ethnic minority students.

Finally, we put forward recommendations to help graduate recruiters address these issues.

Why should a lack of graduate applicants from the ethnic minority population be a worry for graduate recruiters?

Quite simply, the ethnic minority population is becoming an increasing source of skilled and educated labour for employers. To ignore this is to ignore the diversity of expression – in all its respects – such a population brings to the workplace.

The ethnic minority population

The labour supply from the ethnic minority population is set to increase in the future because of:

■ the general growth in the ethnic minority population over time

- the younger age profile of the ethnic minority population compared to the white population
- the increased participation of ethnic minorities in education (higher and full-time) over the last five years.

Growth in the ethnic minority population

The total ethnic minority population in the UK is about 3.3 million, or 5.8 per cent of the total population, representing a gradual increase in size from just under 5 per cent of the population in 1988/89. Prior to that, the ethnic minority population between 1981 and 1990 had increased by 18 per cent.

Younger age profile

The population of the UK, and Europe, is ageing markedly. This means that there will be a decrease in numbers in the younger age groups and a consequent increase in the proportion of older cohorts. Between 1996 and 2001, the number of people of working age over 35 will increase by 1.7 million, or 9 per cent. In contrast, the number of 25–33-year-olds will fall by 1 million, or nearly 11 per cent.

Crucially, the ethnic minority population has a younger age profile than the white population. In the UK, one in every ten adults at present is over 50. While 16 per cent of the UK population is over 65 years of age, ethnic minorities constitute just 1 per cent of this group. Moreover, they make up over 9 per cent of the under-16 age group. Over time, ethnic minority groups will make up a much larger share of the labour force.

Increased participation in higher education

Looking to the future, the number of ethnic minority graduates, at least in the short term, is going to be determined by current trends in participation in further education and by the changes taking place in the higher education system.

Overall, the numbers in full-time education from the 16–24 age group rose by 37 per cent between 1990 and 1996, with a higher proportion of ethnic minority 16–19-year-olds (53.6 per cent) compared to young white people (33.2 per cent). These differences are important for patterns of participation in higher education, and subsequent employment.

In any case, there has been an increasing trend towards greater diversification within student intakes at universities. In 1992 ethnic minority students made up only 8.7 per cent of total applications to universities; in 1996 this had increased to 14 per cent, while by 1999 it was over 17 per cent.

Part of this increase must be attributed to the 1992 reclassification of many polytechnics as universities. Prior to this, ethnic minority students were more likely to be concentrated in polytechnics than in universities. The same is still true today: the majority of ethnic minority students are still to be found in ex-polytechnic institutions, studying vocationally orientated degrees, such as law and finance. To be specific, most of these students tend to be concentrated in a few, less prestigious, institutions, generally ex-polytechnics in London and the Midlands.

Were universities seen as 'white institutions'? Are they still? Perhaps, but the applications data are beginning to suggest otherwise. Not only has the number of ethnic minority applications to universities increased since 1992, but so too have the acceptance rates. In 1992, 53.5 per cent of university applications from white students were accepted, while the figure for ethnic minority students was 26.7 per cent. In 1994, the UCAS admission figures showed that, although there was still a slight disparity in acceptance rates (70 per cent of white applications accepted compared to 63 per cent of ethnic minority applications), the situation was changing considerably, and now is not far off parity, certainly for applicants of Asian origin.

But the concentration of disproportionate numbers in certain kinds of institutions is still to be tackled. A proposal to make the availability of government funds to institutions partly contingent on their attracting a broader range of students should make a difference. Not only would this increase the overall representation of ethnic minority students, but perhaps more importantly, it would also tend to even out their distribution across institutions.

Increased emphasis on equal opportunities and diversity in the workplace

Is it too optimistic to suppose that Britain is now a mature multiracial society? Certainly, there is a continuous growth in the number of employers developing, they would say, active equal opportunity policies. Why are they doing this? Here are some of the reasons they give in their graduate recruitment literature:

■ Mars	'Believe there is a real strength in diversity and welcome graduates from a variety of ethnic backgrounds and cultures'
■ Abbey National	'Good personnel practice'
■ BBC World Service	'Getting better calibre people with valuable new perspectives'
■ Consumers Association	'Fairness and reflecting the society we live in'
■ Prudential	'Important to reflect the diverse population of the UK'
■ Lloyds-TSB	'Applicants from ethnic minorities particularly welcome as they are underrepresented'.

Evidently, some organizations develop equal opportunity policies primarily (they say) for reasons of fairness and good practice. Others pick the potential business benefits of a diverse workforce as the main driver of their policy. Multinational companies are increasingly concerned that their management teams should be reflecting the new reality of a multiracial, multilingual and multicultural global business environment. It is in their interests to attract graduate applicants from the ethnic minority population.

But are they doing enough? Of the 39 organizations advertising themselves in the *Times Top 100* publication, only eight (20 per cent) alluded to anything resembling an equal opportunities policy. An entirely different group of eight mentioned that they had a mentoring scheme. Among those not mentioning a policy or explicitly welcoming applications from ethnic minority graduates were British Airways, British Steel, British Aerospace, Andersen Consulting, PricewaterhouseCoopers, Procter & Gamble, and four City finance houses.

Perhaps the notion of equal opportunities has become *passé*, a flavour-of-the-month concept well past its sell-by date. We ourselves favour what we see as a more inclusive idea – diversity – mentioned by some of those employers like Mars, but equal opportunities in the fundamental sense of equity and parity of treatment and as an engine for the creation and maintenance of a fair society is never *passé*. It looks though as if there is a corporate mindset which says, 'Equal opportunities? Yes, that was the Eighties. We've ticked that one off.' Perhaps they think that we have reached the point of being a mature multiracial society and there is no longer any need to mention ethnic minorities. Perhaps they believe that now they have got the balance of the workforce right, mentoring is the next thing to offer. We can be pretty certain that mentoring would come a long way behind some of the other things ethnic minority students and graduates are looking for, and which we examine next.

What ethnic minority students think of employers

To discover what ethnic minority students think of employers, we conducted research focusing on:

- the important characteristics of potential employers, as perceived by ethnic minority students
- the organizations more and less likely to receive applications from ethnic minority students
- the economic sectors they would like to work in

■ the factors that ethnic minority students think an employer would consider to be attractive or unattractive about them

■ the sources used by ethnic minority students to collect information about organizations.

Approximately 500 students participated in the research. Forty-three per cent of our sample were male, and 57 per cent were female; 59 per cent were white and 41 per cent from ethnic minorities.

Our most significant finding is that there *are* differences: differences between ethnic minority and white students, and between male and female students. These groups differ in:

■ the organizational characteristics they see as important in their decision to make an application

■ the organizations that they are likely to apply to for graduate-level jobs

■ the economic sectors they would like to work in.

Preferred organizational characteristics

Compared to white students, ethnic minority students showed a stronger preference for organizations described as 'an equal opportunity employer', 'protective', 'safe', 'large', 'loyal', 'high-profile', 'professional', 'high-tech' and 'financially secure'. Organizations described as 'stimulating' and 'demanding' were preferred by white students.

Five characteristics were considered to be essential by over 50 per cent of ethnic minority students: 'an equal opportunities employer', 'professional', 'stimulating', 'respectful', and 'financially secure'. However, 'stimulating' was the only organizational characteristic considered to be essential by over 50 per cent of white students.

Female students showed a stronger preference than male students for organizations described as 'an equal opportunity employer'. Significantly, male students did not list 'an equal opportunity employer' in their top ten wanted characteristics. Female students also showed stronger preferences for 'stimulating', 'trusting', 'ethical', 'socially conscious' and 'green' organizations than did male students; males preferred organizations which were 'adventurous', 'high-tech', 'high-profile' and 'large'.

Preferred organizations to apply to

With the proviso that we were working with a list of certain named employers, analysis of the data comparing white and ethnic minority students produced the following results:

■ Ethnic minority students were significantly more likely than white students to consider applying to Glaxo Wellcome, Smith Kline Beecham, British Airways, British Gas, BT, Cadbury Schweppes, Coopers & Lybrand (as was), Boots, W.H. Smith, and Ford Motor Company.

■ Ethnic minority students were more likely than white students to apply to financial services organizations, such as the Halifax, Abbey National, NatWest and Midland. This is also reflected in a stronger preference for working in the banking and finance sector.

■ Ethnic minority students were less likely than white students to apply to public sector organizations. The top ten for ethnic minority students contained no public sector organizations, while for white students there were three (the Foreign Office, the Diplomatic Service and the Department of Education and Employment).

■ Ethnic minority students were less likely than white students to apply to small organizations (that is, those employing less than 50 people).

■ Ethnic minority and female students placed consultancy and professional, communication and media, banking and finance, education and health in their top five sector choices. White students were more diverse in their preferences, including both the government and non-profit-making organizations in their top five.

■ The majority of ethnic minority students in our sample rated 'an equal opportunities employer' as the most important factor when considering making an application. Significantly, fewer white students rated it so highly.

■ Two of the top five factors which would most discourage ethnic minority students from applying to an organization were directly related to equal opportunity issues. They were not having an equal opportunity policy, and having a bad record in implementing equal opportunity policies.

■ Two of the remaining three factors were also related to this issue. Students were wary of applying to small organizations because these were seen as less likely to have a positive stance on equal opportunities issues. Furthermore, they were less likely to apply to organizations with a bad reputation for staff welfare – which could be seen as a more general indicator of poor equal opportunities practice.

■ Ethnic minority students in general consider that their ethnicity is their most unattractive factor to employers. In interviews with ethnic minority students, many issues were raised related to their ethnicity. They found it difficult to tell whether or not discrimination was occurring, saying that it was difficult to 'pin down' the evidence for discrimination. However, they also reported 'just feelings' about discrimination and said that it was 'always in the back of your mind'. This perceived lack of control may explain why ethnic minority students stated a preference for 'protective', 'safe' and 'loyal' employers. These perceptions anticipate difficulties in securing jobs, and have the effect of focusing an applicant's job search on employers thought to be more attentive to equal opportunities.

■ Differences also emerged between ethnic minority and white students on how they gathered information about a prospective employer. While white students relied more on the company recruitment brochure, ethnic minority students made more frequent use of newspapers, the general media, and 'word of mouth' to gather information. We can be pretty sure that one of the reasons they are scanning these sources is to gather information about the equal opportunities reputation of organizations.

■ The ethnic minority students in our sample were very focused on their academic courses. For example, ethnic minority students were keener to find a job relevant to their degree subject.

■ Over 45 per cent of ethnic minority students perceived their qualifications to be most important to employers. By contrast, white students considered their personal qualities and skills to be more important.

Ethnic minority graduates may be mistaken in thinking that organizations are looking only for high grades. If you study what graduate recruiters ask for, it is impossible to miss the importance attached to personal characteristics and abilities such as non-specialist 'managerial' skills, and to interpersonal skills, such as team working, planning and achievement. Our survey on the practice of graduate recruitment and selection revealed that both 'specific personal characteristics' and 'skills' were more influential than 'qualifications' in the employment decision.

Conclusions of our research

From our findings four themes emerge:

■ the significance for ethnic minority students of employers having an equal opportunities policy
■ the impact of organizational image – both corporate and recruitment
■ what students think organizations are looking for in graduates
■ expectations of the recruitment and selection process.

The significance of equal opportunities policies

Many of our interviewees considered that their ethnic origin hindered their employment chances, an observation that is supported by research. For example:

■ Ethnic minority graduates make more applications than white students but gain fewer interviews. The different experiences of the two groups could not be explained by gender, social class or degree result.

■ Ethnic minority students attend more interviews than white students before obtaining a job offer. In their final year, 72.2 per cent of ethnic minority students did not receive job offers, compared to 52.6 per cent of a matched sample of white students.

■ Even though the opportunities for acquiring higher education are becoming more equal, one report concluded that 'there is no likelihood that parity in the market for educational qualifications will bring equality of opportunity in the labour market.'

The conclusion is that ethnic origin was and perhaps still is perceived as the main difficulty in securing employment for ethnic minority students and, when labour opportunities are scarce, it is their perception that they suffer. It is easy to imagine that this could be a prime motivator in wanting to work for an organization that is an authentic equal opportunities employer, one who delivers rather than talks a good game.

The impact of corporate image

The ethnic minority students in our research reported:

■ Not having an equal opportunities policy advertised in the recruitment literature was for them the most off-putting factor in application decisions.

■ Inconsistencies between the equal opportunities content of the recruitment message and the corporate image influenced their application decisions. An infamous example is illustrated below.

Ford Motor Company: the impact of corporate image and recruitment message on application decisions

In February 1996, the Ford Motor Company made a change to an advert, originally used in the UK, for use in the Polish market. This involved changing the colour of ethnic minority employees in the photograph to make them appear white. This poster then somehow came to be used in the UK. The changes were picked up by some of the people shown in the poster and the subsequent story was featured extensively in the news. Prior to this incident our research had indicated that ethnic minority students were significantly more likely than white students to apply to Ford. The following statements made by ethnic minority students in interviews we conducted in February 1996 indicate clearly the negative impact this incident had on potential applications:

■ 'I'm glad I don't have a Ford car.'
■ 'They are a worldwide multinational, they should know better.'
■ 'The recent Ford advert would make me think twice about applying.'

Although Ford's recruitment literature states that it is an equal opportunities employer, the message from the general media clearly questioned this.

This incident highlights the fact that both corporate and recruitment image play a part in attracting applicants to an organization. A negative image may not only restrict the potential graduate applicant pool, but may also affect demand for a company's products and services.

Other examples also illustrate how publicity can raise queries about an organization's commitment to equal opportunities:

No defence for the Army

... The armed forces tend to recruit people who are quite well educated. One set of people are good at one thing but not so good with another. Your Afro-Caribbean is a big chap, often very athletic and more interested in sport and music ... (*Personnel Today*, April 1996)

These remarks were attributed by *The Voice* newspaper to a certain squadron leader. Yet the Ministry of Defence says it is an equal opportunities employer.

The Stephen Lawrence case made everyone aware that police forces are struggling to serve multiracial communities adequately. Part of a recruitment advertisement for West Midlands Police stated: ... so we would like people from all the region's diverse and multi-cultural communities to think about joining us ... Below is some of the publicity surrounding ethnic minorities in the police force:

Ethnic minority officers currently comprise only 1.7% of the police service in England and Wales and 0.2% in Scotland. This under-representation has been repeatedly highlighted in reports from bodies including Her Majesty's Inspectorate of Constabulary (HMIC) and the Commission for Racial Equality (CRE) with calls for action to address the issue. (*Equal Opportunities Review*, July/August 1996)

With just 2.85 per cent of London's police officers coming from ethnic minority backgrounds, the Metropolitan Police still has a long way to go to achieve its aim of becoming more representative of the community it serves. (*People Management*, March 1996)

Many individual police forces are taking positive steps to address the issue of ethnic minority under-representation; however, equality of opportunities in career development and culture will be critical in determining the retention of ethnic minorities within a force once recruited.

The above examples illustrated how discrepancies can arise between what the organization says it does, and what it actually appears to do. According to the ethnic minority students in our sample, there were two main signals from the corporate image which indicated whether an employer practised equal opportunities meaningfully: first, the level of representation of ethnic minority employees and second, the organization's corporate promotional material, and product or services advertisements.

In general, ethnic minority students are wary of how they are viewed by organizations. Interview comments included 'not all companies consider ethnic minorities equally' and 'employers have a certain image of employees – they type-fit'. One factor that appears to influence these judgements is the low visibility of a successful and diverse set of senior managers, for example:

- 'It's harder for us because the dominant colour in organizations is white, and people look for employees who will fit in.'
- 'There has not been one single Asian diplomat in the last five to six years in the Foreign Office.'

'The dominant colour in organizations is white': does this not go to the heart of the matter? Is it not perfectly plausible that the perception of homogeneity could lead to minority applicants not applying to certain organizations? After all, if people different to the norm within that organization have not succeeded, they may not succeed either.

Of course, most organizations will continue to look white, nothing can be done about that; it is the change of ethnic composition and the rate of that change that matters. Meanwhile, the perceived lack of successful ethnic minority senior managers is having an effect on the decisions of young, ambitious, ethnic minority students, a proportion of whom are likely to fall into the high-flyer category.

Apart from the police, there is still under-representation of ethnic minorities in senior levels of the NHS and the social services, and in the Civil Service and the Army. This may go some way to explaining the preference for the private sector expressed by ethnic minority students in our sample. With fewer than 30 black/Asian employees out of 5500 journalists on national newspapers, it may not be surprising that ethnic minority students did not include the communication and media sector among their top five economic sector choices.

Ethnic minority students are specifically advised to examine the way in which an organization advertises its products and services, for example, the extent to which products are marketed to ethnic minority consumers. The assumption is obviously that the value an organization places on its ethnic minority consumers will be taken as a reflection of its belief in the benefits of a diverse workforce, and, furthermore, of its commitment to equal opportunities.

The recruitment message
Ethnic minority students scan recruitment brochures to investigate whether an organization has an equal opportunities policy and if it is evident in their publications, whether there are case studies of ethnic

minority employees, and whether the universities from which the case study employees graduated are not those perceived as being 'traditionally white'.

The recruitment image is also being formed at events such as recruitment and careers fairs. It would appear that presence, or lack of presence, of ethnic minority employees is noted and can be influential in the view that is formed of an organization.

Expectations of the recruitment and selection process

The recruitment and selection process is also important in the messages it conveys about an organization. A transparent recruitment process is important in conveying a positive message. For example, the ethnic minority students in our research perceived that potential employers value their qualifications the most in selection decisions, and that their ethnicity is their most unattractive feature to potential employers.

The following quotes from our research illustrate clearly the impact such beliefs could have on the way ethnic minority undergraduates view an organization's recruitment process:

- 'I have better grades than most of my white classmates and yet I am not getting interviews, nor are my Asian friends.'
- 'I don't know if I have been discriminated against.'
- 'When they see a foreign name on the application form, they favour a British one.'

A little story will illustrate, indeed bear out, the last assertion and what, more generally, will be recognized as 'everyday' discrimination. It concerns what might be called the 'Patel-Evans' problem. A researcher sent speculative letters of application purporting to come from 'applicants' John Evans and Sanjay Patel. The letters went to one hundred top UK companies, perhaps those listed in *The Times Top 100* or a publication very much like it. The upshot was (you've guessed it) that Evans was treated better than Patel. It was not that Patel was badly treated, just that Evans received more favourable treatment, both in quantity and quality of responses.

These statements illustrate how the 'fairness' of the recruitment process is questioned when what is *perceived to be valued* by organizations is not entirely consistent with what is *actually valued* by organizations in selection decisions. Unless informed otherwise, and perhaps not even then, a lack of success in achieving interviews may be perceived as 'unfairness' or 'discrimination' in the process.

For ethnic minority students, the discrepancy between what employers consider to be important and what they actually place emphasis on may inadvertently lead to feelings of 'unfairness' and 'discrimination', even when there is none. For example, if white students with lower grades are called for interview, and ethnic minority students are not, perceptions of injustice may be amplified. Perhaps there is a need for better education among ethnic minority students as to what employers really value in applicants.

Recommendations for organizations wishing to attract applications from ethnic minority students

Our recommendations are clustered in four categories:

- assisting the ethnic minority student population to find out what is on offer
- using the information to tailor your recruitment message
- increasing the transparency of the recruitment and selection process
- raising and enhancing the profile of public sector organizations.

Assisting the ethnic minority student population to find out what is on offer

It seems that ethnic minority students need to be encouraged to make more use of the information resources available to them. Organizations have been set up specifically for ethnic minority undergraduates, for example the Windsor Fellowship, the Junior Afro-Caribbean Chamber of Commerce and the National Mentoring Consortium. The members of these groups give valuable insights into the perceptions of differing ethnic groups, how they view an organization as an employer, what they would like from it as an employer, and whether or not they would apply to the organization for employment and why.

Practically all universities have numerous societies and clubs for individuals of similar ethnic backgrounds. Their members would probably be very interested in talking to employers who actually value their opinions and are seeking their applications. Approaching these clubs and societies would also give organizations an opportunity to demonstrate their commitment to equal opportunities and to managing diversity.

Using the information to tailor your recruitment message

Some actions organizations can take include:

- Advertise your commitment to equal opportunities through specific statements in your recruitment literature. Whilst such statements are not necessarily taken as fact, their absence could be taken as a reflection of a lack of commitment to equal opportunities. Indeed, the Commission for Racial Equality in its Code of Practice recommends that 'in order to demonstrate their commitment to equality of opportunity it is recommended that where employers send literature to applicants, this should include a statement that they are equal opportunity employers.'
- Examine organizational publicity with regard to equal opportunities and ascertain the messages that are being conveyed: do they demonstrate that actions taken internally are consistent with stated policies and organizational values?
- Organizations should aim to portray their commitment to equal opportunities in a positive light. Thus, if media attention has been negative, they need to counteract this image if they wish to attract a diversity of applicants.
- Ensure that the process of attracting applicants to the organization is in accordance with best practice standards (see the Appendix).
- Organizations need to monitor continually the equal opportunity messages they are projecting as their influence in attracting applications from ethnic minority undergraduates should not be underestimated.

Action is also needed to ensure the 'transparency' of the recruitment process:

- Selection criteria should be sent to all potential applicants who express an interest. Ensure that potential applicants are aware of the link between the qualifications required and the competences needed.
- Information should be requested from applicants for monitoring purposes (sex, race, disability, age).
- Ensure that you regularly review and audit your process to ascertain that it is fair and in line with best practice standards.

Improving the profile of public sector organizations

Public sector organizations need to focus on counteracting or even dispelling assumptions made about their approach to equal opportunities. For example:

- The fact that the public sector has higher proportions of ethnic minorities in top positions needs to be capitalized on by actively publicizing that these people are in place.

- Likewise, the diversity of the organization at all levels (where that claim can be made) should be illustrated more prominently within the recruitment and corporate literature.
- PR publicity and the media could be used more effectively to highlight the existing diversity within the organization as evidence to applicants that the organization's actions are consistent with the policies it says it values.

Key points from this chapter

- In future, ethnic minority graduates will represent a significantly larger percentage of the labour supply than in the recent past. Yet many organizations report that ethnic minorities do not apply to them in the same proportions as white graduates.
- Though a concentration of disproportionate numbers of ethnic minority students in certain kinds of institutions still exists, the trend is towards more even distribution across institutions.
- In an increasingly multiracial, multilingual and multicultural global business environment, it is in the interests of employers to attract graduate applicants from the ethnic minority population.
- Some large employers may become complacent about equal opportunities but equal opportunities in the fundamental sense of equity and parity of treatment and as an engine for the creation and maintenance of a fair society is never *passé*.
- Compared to white students, ethnic minority students show a stronger preference for organizations described as 'an equal opportunity employer', 'protective', 'safe', 'large', 'loyal', 'high-profile', 'professional', 'high-tech' and 'financially secure'.
- Ethnic minority students are more likely than white students to apply to financial services organizations, and less likely to apply to public sector organizations.
- Two factors which most discourage ethnic minority students from applying to an employer are the lack of an equal opportunity policy and having a bad record in implementing equal opportunity policies.
- Ethnicity is still perceived as the main difficulty in securing employment for ethnic minority students and when labour opportunities are scarce they suffer. This is likely to be a prime motivator in wanting to work for a proven equal opportunities employer.
- Though evidence of skills rather than degree class is already weighted more heavily by the more forward-thinking organizations, ethnic minority students have not yet fully realized this.
- Low visibility, or total absence, of a successful and diverse set of senior managers is a big turn-off for ethnic minority graduates when scrutinizing an organization.

■ The public sector, in particular, needs to capitalize on the fact that it has higher proportions of ethnic minorities in top positions.

Managing the applicant pool

Graduate recruiters continue to worry over the number of graduate applications they receive, and the extent to which these applicants are suitable to be recruited into the organization. In practice, the occurrence of large applicant pools containing many unsuitable applicants appears to be seen as a logistical problem to be responded to rather than something over which control can be exerted. Where you stand on this issue is crucial. If you do not address it you will find that your recruitment procedures will become progressively less effective and efficient.

The benefits of effective and efficient recruitment for organizations can be listed as follows:

- less time and money spent on recruitment
- quicker results
- reduced turnover
- same results with fewer people
- better results from better people
- substandard people quickly replaced
- penalty costs of bad practice avoided or contained.

Number of graduate applicants

The number of graduates has increased dramatically. Given the growth in participation in higher education, this trend looks set to continue for the immediate future. Larger applicant pools mean more money and time spent on recruitment processes. Some research we did in 1997 revealed that 46 per cent of public sector organizations and 45 per cent of those in the private sector received over 750 graduate applications per year (see Table 5.1). One legal firm was quoted as receiving over 3,000 graduate applications for just 25 vacancies, while Ernst and Young, a Big Six accountancy firm which recruits approximately 450 graduates per year, received over 6,000 graduate applications.

Table 5.1   Number of graduate applications per year by public and private sector organizations

Number of graduate applications per year	% of public sector organizations	% of private sector organizations
Up to 250	22	36
251–750	32	19
More than 750	46	45

Our research indicated that 72 per cent of organizations offer jobs to only 5 per cent or less of initial graduate applicants. On average, each private sector organization recruits 25 graduates per year, but each public sector organization recruits over 50 graduates per year.

A consequence of the growing applicant pool is the longer time taken to process and screen graduate applications. This not only impacts upon the organization in terms of time and resources, but also in terms of the recruitment message it projects. Thirty-seven per cent of organizations reported that their process of recruiting and selecting graduates took over four months. Over a third of students had waited between three to four weeks for an initial response to their application. More to the point, less than a tenth were satisfied with this speed of response. If graduates were customers (which they are), no organization would be satisfied with such ratings.

The larger the applicant pool becomes, the more costly, time-consuming and difficult it becomes to screen out the unsuitable applicants, and the more likely it is that the more suitable applicants have already taken alternative employment. In law and accountancy, for example, firms are gazumping each other for high-flying recruits.

Some organizations complain that, even with large applicant pools, they often do not attract sufficient numbers of suitable applications. Many of the applicants do not have the skills or qualities they are seeking. Organizations which require specialist skills – and which do not? – are not just competing with organizations from their own sector. Higher salaries are attracting graduates to general management or consultancy positions rather than to jobs where they could apply their specialist skills.

Management consultancy is indeed the hot spot – or is it honeypot? It was the leading destination for graduates in 1999, with as many as one in seven graduates looking for jobs attracted to management consultancy. The top graduate employers in 1999 were Andersen Consulting, Arthur Andersen, and PricewaterhouseCoopers. Next were Procter & Gamble and the Civil Service. Other employers who appear among the top ten (of *The Times* 100) were British Airways, Marks & Spencer, KPMG, Unilever and Boots.

The City is also attractive, especially to mathematicians (who are targeted as financial analysts, derivatives traders and so on). In fact, any kind of scientist with presumed analytical nous can be attractive to the banking world. Remember the Cambridge graduate with a degree in astrophysics who landed a job as a Wall Street trader: the banks are willing to pay top dollar for instant brains.

Getting graduates to apply

A crucial stage in designing an effective graduate selection process is to choose the method or methods by which graduates can apply to your organization. You will need to weigh up carefully the different methods that are available and make best use of these. Below, we look at application forms, CVs and speculative applications, and the Internet.

Application forms

Our research has shown that the most commonly used method by which graduates are asked to apply to an organization is through an application form. Employers see it as the second most influential tool in the selection process after the interview. By its content, style and layout, the application form is obviously communicating an important message about the organization, not always, it must be said, the one the organization wants to communicate.

Important it may be but only a minority of graduate recruiting organizations take a systematic approach to designing the application form. Without special design, application forms are not well suited to shortlisting. Yet enormous emphasis is placed on these forms because they are the basis for screening out large numbers of applicants.

If you use an application form as a screening tool, then you are using it as a selection device. The novel approach of Asda, the supermarket chain, makes the point. It asks graduates to complete a questionnaire on-line, the success of which will determine whether they are allowed to proceed to the next stage of actually completing an on-line application form. If rejected at this stage, applicants are given the Internet addresses of Asda's competitors such as Tesco and Sainsburys.

The information given by graduates in standard application forms is likely to be fairly similar, with most having similar backgrounds and experiences, and relatively little in the way of related work experience. Accordingly, employers need to find ways to differentiate fairly and effectively between graduate applicants. They need to identify what qualities they are looking for and design the form around these. Beyond that, employers need to introduce or sustain transparency in their process, and offer applicants the opportunity for self-selection; in other words, to exclude themselves. Two different kinds of application forms help to do this: competency-based and biodata.

Competency-based application forms

Competencies are the behaviours that individuals need to display in order to do a job effectively. To identify the competencies required for successful job performance, a thorough job analysis is required. This can be achieved using a variety of methods, including observation, diaries, interviews, critical incident technique, repertory grid and checklists/inventories. The choice of method will depend upon timescales, budgets, size of the relevant population, and so on.

From job analysis comes a number of behavioural incidents which will exemplify good and poor performance in a particular competency. Behavioural incidents require context (the situation requiring the person to act), action (what an individual said or did in response to the situation), and outcome (the result of the person's actions). By eliciting these incidents, questions for an application form can easily be compiled.

The questions in a competency-based application form are designed in a way that asks applicants to give evidence in order to demonstrate the competency required. This evidence should come directly from an applicant's experience, and should be illustrated by examples of context, action and outcome. Table 5.2 provides some examples of competency-based questions used in current graduate recruitment forms.

The advantages of competency-based application forms are that:

■ They provide structure so that information is presented in a uniform way.
■ The examples that are given as evidence can be used as the basis for further probing at the interview stage.
■ The competencies identified are only those that affect actual job performance, so the likelihood of bias based on selecting for irrelevant characteristics, such as gender or ethnicity, is reduced.
■ It is relatively simple to screen applications – a rating scale can be devised to mark the forms, and sift out the best applicants.

The disadvantages of competency-based application forms are that:

■ They are open-ended, therefore an organization may not get the kind of information that it is looking for. (This can be overcome by encouraging the candidate to be specific by asking several questions.)
■ Marking the competency-based form can be a tedious and time-consuming process (but there are ways of mitigating the task).

Table 5.2   Examples of competency-based questions

Competency	Sample question
Drive and initiative	Describe two ambitions leading to recent achievements which demonstrated your determination to complete challenging tasks.
Interpersonal skills	Describe a situation in which you had to influence other people. What did you say, what were their objections, and how did you overcome them?
Problem-solving	Think of a problem that you have had to resolve. How did you go about finding a solution? What did you learn in the process?
Leadership	Please give an example of a situation where you led a group of people. Try to include: what the group was trying to achieve, the number of people in the group, why you were appointed the leader, and how you dealt with the different members of the group.

Biodata forms

Biodata – biographical accounts of past events – is information concerning an individual's personal life history and experience. It encompasses wider aspects than just behaviour alone, such as personality and motivation. The data are then used to predict the likely future performance of an applicant in the job. Table 5.3 provides some examples of biodata-based questions found in graduate application forms.

To construct a biodata questionnaire, a thorough job analysis needs to be undertaken in order to decide what abilities, competencies, skills and traits are required for superior performance in the job. Then testable hypotheses about the biographical determinants of the skills derived from the job analysis need to be generated. The more time spent analysing the job, and the nature of successful and less successful jobholders in the past, the more sensitive and accurate are the hypotheses generated. Examples of testable hypotheses would be:

- 'Having strong religious beliefs (regardless of what the religion is) is associated with organizational commitment.'
- 'Hobbies of a cognitive nature such as computers, chess, and bridge are associated with numerical ability and preference.'

■ 'Evidence of enthusiastic participation in team sports is associated with managerial skills.'

Specific biodata items can be chosen from catalogues or previous studies, and tailored to suit the organization. They can also be developed internally, for example, questionnaires on lifestyle and personality completed by a sample of employees will indicate common traits shared by high performers. An application form can then be designed which will pick out applicants who appear to share similar characteristics.

The questions are usually multiple-choice, and an objective scoring system is used to mark the responses. Generally, biodata produces a simple score that enables recruiters to identify those applicants likely to be best suited to the job.

Table 5.3   Examples of biodata-based questions

Sample biodata questions	
When you take a holiday, do you prefer:	
To plan all the details in advance	❏
To make general plans only	❏
To be as spontaneous as possible	❏
To stay at home or on familiar ground	❏
Which of these descriptions best fits you?	
I read a great deal on many subjects	❏
I read mostly about things related to my work	❏
I haven't much time for reading, but read as much as I can	❏
About the only reading I manage is the newspaper	❏
I usually have better things to do than to sit about reading	❏

The advantages of biodata are that:

■ It is cost-effective, especially if multiple-choice questions and machine scoring are utilized.
■ It is easy to mark, given that the standards set in using biodata questionnaires are objective and consistent, so that consistency between raters is guaranteed.

The disadvantages of biodata (and they are considerable) are that:

■ It provides no explanation of why some factors are more significant than others in presaging high performance. If it says that successful sales people are good at sports, you have to go along with it, whatever your private opinion. This is called, in the trade, 'blind empiricism'.
■ Applicants can easily fake replies to biodata questions to suit the organization's requirements.
■ Biodata causes concern in terms of equal opportunities. Questions about age, sex, disability, and ethnic background are contentious issues and could be deemed illegal if a selection decision was based on them.
■ Biodata also raises some concern about homogeneity. If a great deal of biodata-based information is used in selection, an organization will inevitably become more homogeneous over time. This is sometimes called the 'cloning' problem. If certain criteria on which most staff have been chosen no longer predict success, then an organization has no option but to abandon biodata, or go through the whole development process again if it thinks it is worth it (which it probably will not).

CVs and speculative applications

Speculative letters that are sent to organizations enquiring about the possibility of a job usually include the applicant's CV. Applicants can always decide what to put into their CVs, whereas in an application form the organization maintains control over what it specifically requires. In this sense, it is more difficult for an organization to screen a CV and/or a speculative application. It is becoming increasingly common for individuals to structure their CV around competencies, but these competencies are not necessarily the ones that organizations are interested in.

Employers who are keen to promote equal employment opportunities, notably those in the public sector, are more likely to reject the CV as a method of application. In addition, many large organizations (especially those which receive thousands of applications), do not accept speculative letters as a method of application. They reply to speculative letters by sending back an application form, and ask applicants to fill this in instead. As long as they explain that the application form is part of their regular procedure, and is necessary for legal reasons, candidates usually respond without hesitation.

The use of CVs may increase greatly in the future as a growing number of electronic CV-scanning products are now available. Optical character recognition (OCR) software is used to scan the CV and convert the scanned material into basic text format. Most high-tech products have artificial intelligence to read the text and extract key data. Artificial intelligence enables the system to recognize skills and qualifications, regardless of how well they are presented on paper. The computer can reorganize the information into a summary for the user, and match skills and qualifications to vacancies throughout the organization. Where there are no matches, the system can hold information and compare it with new positions that arise.

The issue still remains one of consistency, however. The more skilled or practised someone is at writing a CV the more chance they will have of being shortlisted. Whilst new technology offers great potential in helping organizations deal with the laborious task of sifting through thousands of application forms, it has yet to be thoroughly tried and tested.

The Internet

The use of the Internet as a means of attracting graduate applications is increasing greatly, probably exponentially. The advantage for organizations is that accessing the Net is much faster and significantly cheaper than paper media, and all information is produced and stored automatically on the computer. For students, the advantages are similar – they can apply directly via the screen, and they have access to the Net via university facilities. However, robust links are needed and technology still needs to become quicker and easier to use.

Our interviews with graduate recruiters suggested that, whilst most organizations had not formally evaluated the Internet as a form of graduate recruitment, many felt that it was an area where further developments would continue to occur. This was mainly due to the growth of the international market, the need to target students outside the UK and the need to maintain a competitive profile.

One manufacturing organization's goal for graduate recruitment by the year 2000 was to have 'Internet recruitment with a dedicated web site which would include the company brochure and an application form'. It saw the advantages of this approach as including:

- ■ A wider range of students have access to information about their organization.
- ■ It reduces costs as they do not have to produce a paper graduate brochure.

- It means they can easily update information about candidates and the organization.
- They can advertise vacancies much more quickly and regularly.
- Students can find out more about the organization before assessment.
- The organization can recruit graduates internationally.

Presently (though the situation is changing fast), the majority of organizations do not directly ask for graduate applications via the Internet, but there are now a number of dedicated graduate Internet sites which advertise job vacancies, and which hold CVs or biographical data for companies to sift through.

The law firm Eversheds uses its website to recruit graduates using innovative and interactive tactics to attract what it describes as 'job seeking traffic'. By including a competition, with a prize of a week's paid work experience in its Paris office, Eversheds has offered an incentive to visit its website, the intention being that once there, individuals might take the time to complete an online application form.

The trend of utilizing the Internet as a recruitment medium is undoubtedly growing. Research in the UK suggests that just under 50 per cent of UK companies are using the Internet for recruitment purposes. Market research projections predict that the majority of medium and large US organizations will utilize Web-based recruiting by 2002. Figures from Ireland suggest an increase in Internet use by 300 per cent in the last two years, and that, by 2005, 41 per cent of the population will be using the Net. A survey by Incomes Data Services of 1999 graduate recruitment practice reported a growth in the number of companies using the Internet to advertise for and to recruit graduates.

Given this growth rate, what proof is there that there is any measurable gain for companies? While promotional material from companies claim that the Internet provides the opportunity to cut costs and increase the efficiency of the entire hiring process, there has been to date minimal research conducted on the validity and utility of using the Internet for recruitment.

Let us try to summarize why the Net is attractive for hiring. It is a global medium; it reaches an additional set of candidates; it is unbounded by geography and time, and it allows more scope to promote the company. In an increasingly global market, where competition for candidates is high, and there is a shortage of skilled candidates for technology jobs, the Net is seen as an attractive recruitment medium.

However, some of the methodological concerns include:

- Demographic skew among Internet users could result in 'applicant flow problems'.
- Web-based selection requires at least the same degree of careful validation that traditional techniques entail.

■ The uncontrolled nature of Web interactions may create substantial opportunities for faking and cheating.

■ The collection of personnel information such as test scores and biographical data over the Net raises some security and personal privacy concerns that need to be addressed.

Unequal opportunities on the World Wide Web

In the US, the majority of Internet users tend to be white, male and younger than 40. Corresponding survey figures from Ireland suggest that 68 per cent of Internet users are male and that 70 per cent have third-level education. The typical Irish Internet user is aged 35, male, third level, and earns on average £30,000.

At the present time, Web-based recruiting may be appropriate only for a limited set of positions that correspond strongly with regular use of computers on the job. The demographic skew and the technical bent of the on-line job market interact to worsen the EO picture. Minorities and women are under-represented in highly technical fields and are under-represented in the pool of Internet users. For all these reasons, organizations should avoid using the Net as the sole medium for recruiting unless the recruiting is very targeted.

The importance of equal opportunity monitoring

Equal opportunity monitoring is a key aspect of best practice that should be built into the design of any application form. Reasons for requesting monitoring information should be given on the form, as well as a guide as to how the information will and will not be used.

Without monitoring the number of applications received from different groups of individuals, organizations cannot be sure that their attraction or selection processes are not having an adverse impact on certain groups. It is therefore disturbing that our research showed that almost 40 per cent of organizations in our sample did not conduct any form of monitoring whatsoever. What is even more disappointing is that some organizations which do conduct equal opportunity monitoring do not actually make any use of their data. In this respect, monitoring must go beyond headcount if it is to yield any information about the effects of particular practices and procedures.

Summary of the advantages and disadvantages of different application methods

The choice of application method is dependent upon various factors which include the number of applications you are likely to receive, the amount of time and resources you have available for screening and short-listing, and the budget you have available. Table 5.4 illustrates the advantages and disadvantages of the different application methods that we have discussed.

Table 5.4 Advantages and disadvantages of different application methods

Application method	Advantages	Disadvantages
Competency -based form	■ Provides structure so that information is presented in a uniform way ■ Examples can be used as the basis for interviews ■ A rating scale can be devised to mark these forms	■ It is open-ended, therefore you may not get the type of information you are looking for ■ Marking can be a tedious and time-consuming process
Biodata-based form	■ Can be multiple-choice, so is easy to mark ■ Can be marked by machines/computers ■ Is cost-effective	■ Scoring is empirically based, hence large sample sizes are needed ■ Causes concern for equal opportunities ■ Can be prone to faking problems
CVs/ speculative applications	■ Cheaper than producing application forms ■ Useful for smaller organizations that do not have many graduate vacancies ■ CV-scanning software is now available	■ May tell you nothing about an applicant's suitability for the job ■ Presents difficulties in marking and screening ■ An organization has no control over it
Internet applications	■ It is quicker than paper media ■ It can be cheaper than paper media ■ Information is stored automatically on the screen ■ Graduates have easy access to the Internet at universities/ colleges ■ Access to international graduates	■ Robust, high-speed links are needed ■ Technology needs to become quicker and easier to use ■ Not all students may know how to use the Internet

Screening applications

Many organizations complain about the sheer volume of applications they receive for only a small number of graduate positions. Public sector organizations, such as the fire and police services, and the most popular graduate recruiters, all attract applications in large numbers. The police, for example, receive 60,000–80,000 applications each year for 5,000–6,000 positions as probationer constables. Where numbers like these are involved, applying the principle of 'I'll know it when I see it' falls woefully short of the mark.

To sift through thousands of forms efficiently it is vital to know what information you are looking for, and to be able to get to it easily. Building the application form around competencies is an important first step.

To speed up the sifting process significantly, you also need a marking scheme, or set of decision rules, which enables quick decisions to be made about applications. Where numbers are high, using a properly structured form, it should be possible to reject applicants as soon as they fail a hurdle and before marking of the form is complete. This immediate discard technique can save a great deal of time and money. In practice, the discard rule is unlikely to be as severe as this, and will usually depend on the ratio of applicants to jobs available. But what matters most is that criteria be applied consistently – if not, you risk compromising the utility of the system precisely at the point where you have the widest diversity of talent to choose from.

The advantages of adopting this kind of approach become more apparent when the results of a survey of 536 high-volume recruiters are considered. Ninety-four per cent indicated that application forms were used to screen out applicants, although the proportion who were rejected using this method varied. At one extreme, 30 per cent of organizations screened out less than one in three. At the other, 15 per cent rejected more than seven out of ten applicants. In this situation, one needs to be very confident of the validity of the application form as a screen and of the skill of the people doing the sifting.

In the same survey a disturbing 82 per cent of organizations failed to provide any guidelines for screeners on how to interpret the information on the application form, and only just over half provided them with any formal training. Specially designed forms were used by only half the organizations questioned, and of these only 14 had carried out any kind of pilot study.

What concerns us about these results is the damage organizations are doing to their chances of landing the best recruits: the majority of rejections are made using off-the-shelf or untested application forms and asking untrained people to make the decisions.

The implications of leaving sifters to their own devices are not entirely comforting. One study, in which those making the decisions were asked to think aloud, paints a bleak picture. It revealed that sifters tend to make assumptions about personality, motivation and job knowledge from the information they were given, rather than use the information itself. Significantly more weight is given to negative information, as also tends to be the case with other selection methods including interviews and references. Rather than look for evidence for specific criteria (such as competencies) they make general judgements with all of the problems of prejudice that entails.

Active screening

Screening is about selecting the most promising from a mass of applicants. It is sifting the wheat from the chaff. Consequently, special care needs to be given to the screening process because if it is carried out inefficiently the correct selection decisions will not be made. Here we examine criteria for effective screening, and different approaches to screening that organizations use.

Criteria for effective screening

Construct a marking scheme

One of the key methods of screening applications effectively is to construct a strategy in the form of a rating scheme. The strategy should be based upon the specific criteria that you are looking for in a graduate. Therefore, it makes sense to design the marking scheme at the same time you design the application form.

In a competency-based application form, each question is designed to elicit evidence on one particular criterion. In the screening process evidence given by an applicant is matched to specific behavioural indicators that are required. These indicators have already been established from the job analysis and behavioural interviews carried out with high performers already in the job. Table 5.5 contains an example of a rating scheme used by some organizations.

At times this method of screening can be time-consuming and extremely hard work, but it is essential that all applications are sifted using a consistent approach.

Once an application form has been marked, a decision needs to be made as to whether the applicant should be shortlisted or not. Another set of rules can be applied here also. For example:

■ Applicants who score no Cs should be invited to a preliminary interview.
■ Applicants who score only one C should be put on hold for a period of one month.

■ Applicants who score two or more Cs should be immediately discarded.

If by applying the shortlisting rule you are left with more applicants than it is practical to handle at the next stage of the selection process, secondary shortlisting should be carried out by applying a more stringent rule, for example, of the eight competencies being assessed the ratings should be at least six As and two Bs. This rule must be applied consistently for all applicants.

We mentioned the immediate discard technique. For this to work efficiently, competencies must be presented in a particular order, starting with those most closely related to the overall job performance. Job analysis will yield some clues to the most appropriate sequence, as will any previous validation work. For example, in one particular project where six competencies were covered on the application form, a pilot exercise allowed us to determine how competencies correlated with performance and therefore, the running order which would produce the most efficient sift.

By strictly applying the immediate discard technique, the sifting process can be carried out quickly. Knocking out applicants on the first or second competency would take no longer than a minute. An application form which includes a relatively large number of competencies (six, for example) will also act as a screen given that speculative applicants tend to be put off by the sheer size of the task. Our own experience is that whilst the number of returns is reduced, the quality of candidates remains high.

Without immediate discard – you may prefer to score the whole form anyway, or have no grounds for ranking competencies – it will take three minutes to sift a form with four competencies. Timescales can be cut

Table 5.5 Example of a rating scheme

'A' ratings	■ Strong evidence ■ The answer is clear and directly answers the questions asked ■ The answer contains a large number of the indicators (two-thirds or more)
'B' ratings	■ Acceptable evidence ■ The answer gives an indication that evidence is present, but it is a little vague and needs to be explored more at interview ■ The answer contains some indicators (approximately half)
'C' ratings	■ Poor evidence/lack of evidence ■ The answer does not relate to the question ■ The answer contains few indicators (one or two)

further by first sifting against any stringent technical requirements, for example fluency in a foreign language. In each case, it is strongly recommended that those doing the sifting receive the necessary training and that forms are double marked to ensure consistency.

It is estimated that based on a six-competency form it would take around six hours to sift 200 completed applications, discard 80 per cent and leave 20 per cent to go on to the next stage of recruitment. Compared with the cost of hiring unsuitable people, many organizations will find this approach makes sound economic sense. Whilst there are more patently obvious criteria – the colour of the ink used, whether the writing is neat, or whether applicants cross their sevens – the extra effort applied at the point when you have the most people to choose from will undoubtedly pay dividends later.

Use of reference material

Our research findings indicate that almost all organizations collect reference letters at some stage of the application process: the majority are collected as a final check *after* a conditional offer has been made. This is felt by some to be a potentially confusing approach. Obviously there is potentially valuable information which could be used earlier in the selection process.

There are legal dangers involved in providing and seeking references, especially with regard to the risks of negligence. There has been at least one case where an employee sued his former employer for writing what he regarded as slighting or damaging remarks. References therefore need to be used with particular caution, especially if they make the difference between an applicant securing employment or not (they shouldn't).

References rank rather low in terms of validity coefficients (that is, not much better than handwriting) which again emphasizes the dangers involved in using them. Improvements could be made in the use of reference checks by treating them as structured interviews. Regardless of the methods used to obtain references, employers should ask for *facts* about the applicant, for example, the number of days they were absent in the past year, or if there had been any reason to give them an official warning. Facts like these are much more useful than seeking *opinions* about someone's performance.

Training

Thorough training must be given to all those involved in the screening and shortlisting process. Given the practical importance of effective screening, it is surprising that as many as 35 per cent of private sector organizations in our research sample gave no training to individuals in the screening of application forms/CVs. Organizations may take the view that it is not crucial to screen effectively if they 'get it right' at the selection stage, but this ignores the fact that selection outcomes are influenced by earlier decisions. These early screening decisions determine the quality of the shortlisted pool of applicants, hence training for those involved in making these decisions is vital.

Different approaches to screening

Organizations use a variety of approaches to screen graduate applicants, ranging from an in-house team dedicated to screening to outsourcing agencies that will conduct the screening for them. The advantages and disadvantages of each approach will vary depending on the organization.

Some organizations, especially large accountancy and consulting firms, are now conducting some form of pre-screening *before* they send out application forms. For example, one employer we interviewed requires graduates to phone them in order to request an application form. When they phone up, they are asked how many points (or equivalent) they have from their A-level grades. Only if graduates have a certain number of UCCA points which is equal to or greater than a cut-off value will they be sent an application form.

The advantage of this approach is that graduates are aware from the outset that it is not worth applying to the organization unless they meet certain criteria (that is, high A-level grades), so their time is not wasted by filling out an application form. Similarly, for the organization there will be a reduction in the number of 'unsuitably qualified' graduates applying from the outset, which makes screening easier. This approach is also likely to be more cost-effective for them. The organization is, of course, making the assumptions that graduates with high A-level grades are likely to perform the graduate role more effectively than those with lower grade. Potentially significantly from an equal opportunities point of view, there is actually no evidence linking low A-level grades to lower job performance, so using them as a screen could be excluding potentially suitable applicants. Then, there are the PR implications: the organization may be portrayed negatively by those graduates with lower UCCA points who were not sent the application form.

A growing number of organizations outsource screening to cope with the vast number of applications they receive, and a growing number use new technology to make screening easier. A number of recruitment agencies are now set up specifically to deal with enquiry calls, send out application forms, and do the initial screening of applicants. The advantage of this for organizations is a massive saving of time and resources.

The two examples below illustrate some of these different approaches to screening. Whatever method is used it is essential that:

- The criteria used are relevant.
- The process is standardized.

■ The shortlisters follow the process in an objective and systematic way.

Screening in a large retail organization

Enquiries for application forms are dealt with via a free phone information number, which is connected to an external agency. The agency sends out the application forms, but applicants have to return completed forms to the head office of this retail organization.

■ Around 14,000 applications are received each year (from both graduates and non- graduates), and approximately 30 per cent of these get to the next stage of assessment. The application forms are competency-based, so they can be scored. Each completed application form is scanned onto a computerized database.

■ The computer is able to read the application forms, score them and produce a report based on individuals' scores. Staff will then read the report and form their decisions as to who will be asked to go on to the next stage of assessment. The computer can automatically generate rejection or 'next-stage' letters which are sent to applicants.

■ The advantages of this approach, as seen by the organization, are that it is speedy, accurate and provides equal opportunities monitoring.

■ Speculative applicants are asked to fill out application forms, and all CVs are returned.

Screening in a large manufacturing organization

■ This organization receives approximately 4,000 to 5,000 applications every year, and offers 80 to 100 positions.

■ External consultants are used to mark the application forms, using a specific strategy. The strategy looks at individuals' grades at A level, their likely degree result, their related work experience, and extra-curricular activities that the applicant has undertaken.

■ The criteria outlined above are weighted by the organization, and those who exceed a required cut-off score are passed on to the relevant departments for consideration for a further interview.

■ The managers in the relevant departments look for certain criteria in the application forms, and assess them against the types of people and experience they require.

Deterring the unsuitable candidate

Some people are put off from applying for a job simply because they must fill in an application form, others drop out when they understand what the whole application process involves.

Communicating what the job will actually entail, warts and all, through a Realistic Job Preview (RJP) is also an effective way of cutting down applications and the cost of recruitment. An RJP can be sent out with the application form and works on the principle that given enough information about the job people will assess their prospects realistically and unsentimentally and screen themselves in or out.

A Realistic Job Preview can be designed either to enhance overly pessimistic expectations or, as is more often the case, to reduce overly optimistic expectations. It can also be communicated through the job description, a brochure, application pack, an interview or an advertisement.

Key points from this chapter

- The occurrence of large applicant pools containing many unsuitable applicants appears to be seen as a logistical problem to be responded to rather than something over which control can be exerted, but control *can* be exerted.
- To sift thousands of forms efficiently it is vital to know what information you are looking for, and to be able to get to it easily. Building the application form around competencies is an important first step.
- Where numbers are high, a properly structured form makes it possible to reject applicants as soon as they fail a hurdle and before marking of the form is complete.
- Discard criteria must be applied consistently, otherwise the utility of the system is compromised precisely at the point where the diversity of talent to choose from is at its greatest.
- If sifters are left to their own devices they tend to make assumptions about personality, motivation and job knowledge from the information they were given, rather than use the information itself.
- Deterring the unsuited is a crucial part of exerting control over the applications process. Communicating what the job will actually entail, through a Realistic Job Preview is an effective way of cutting down applications and the cost of recruitment.

Selection methods

The graduates have applied, you have screened them – Now you must select those you want. How to do this is the subject of this chapter. First, though, we must re-visit *recruitment-relevant competencies* because they bind everything together.

Recruitment-relevant competencies

New graduates usually have limited work experience or work-related skills. Organizations therefore need to be specific in the competencies against which they wish to assess graduates. These competencies should be *recruitment-relevant,* that is the competencies that are required to perform the job *immediately*. As such, they are a 'need to have' rather than a 'nice to have'. The 'nice to have' competencies can be acquired once the graduate has started working, through training and development.

So how do you go about identifying recruitment-relevant competencies for graduates? The following case study illustrates one approach to take.

A multinational organization

We conducted interviews with individuals who were on the graduate development programme of a large multinational organization. They ranged from graduates who had been with the organization for three months to those who had been there for three years. We wanted to find out from these people what, having worked in the organization, they thought were the essential qualities needed to succeed.

We also talked to senior managers to find out how the organization was changing and what this meant in terms of the qualities that needed to be sought in the graduate applicants of today. Departmental heads and function specialists were also interviewed to find out what technical skills were required.

The interviews focused on the skills and qualities graduates would need to undertake their role *immediately*. They also focused on the differences between successful and less successful graduates. The interviews also helped us to discover what qualities were going to be needed in the senior managers of the future.

Information collected from these interviews was used to compile a questionnaire, which asked managers and graduates to prioritize a range of behaviours. Managers were asked whether the competencies were a 'need to have' on entry, or whether they could be developed. They were also asked to prioritize and rank-order these competencies. Out of this information came the recruitment-relevant competencies. Having them meant that a selection process could be devised which could be tailored specifically to recruit high-calibre graduates.

The various assessment methods

There follows a description of the various assessment methods available to the graduate recruiter, with requirements, advantages and downsides, and new developments (where we think there are any) itemized.

Role-plays

Role-plays are one-to-one exercises where the candidate conducts an interview or meeting with a role-player, who has been given a thorough briefing. The role-play is observed by an assessor or assessors (though it can be videotaped). The assessor may question the candidate afterwards to find out more about the strategy, direction and outcome of the interview/meeting.

Requirements
Role-plays require

■ skilled role-players and assessors
■ role-players responding consistently to all candidates.

Advantages of role-plays
Role-plays have the advantages of:

■ allowing observation of 'people skills',
■ being realistic, especially for managerial tasks, and
■ can be tailored to suit a range of tasks and situations.

Downsides
The worst disadvantage is that candidates may feel that they have been put in a false situation, that is, they lack the background knowledge from which to determine tactics. Role-plays are also unpopular with under-

graduates who tend to complain that if they had wanted to be actors they would have done so.

New development
The interesting development these days is the use of professional role-players, usually actors, to play roles opposite the candidate. It has been our experience that candidates are invariably bowled over by what these actors bring to the assessment situation and this, in itself, contributes greatly to validating the assessment for candidates.

Group discussions

In a group discussion, between four and eight candidates are given a short case study or management problem. They are asked to resolve the problem and/or make recommendations, sometimes in writing. The group is given a fixed time to reach conclusions. Assessors are assigned to observe and record the contributions of specific group members.

Basically, there are two types of group discussion:

■ Assigned roles – People are not all given the same brief; some elements of the brief will be common to all and some elements will be individual.
■ Non-assigned roles – All people are given the same brief.

Requirements
For a successful and informative group discussion, assessors need highly developed observation skills.

Advantages of group discussions
A group discussion will:

■ enable assessment of people interacting with each other
■ allow candidates to reveal characteristics they may not be fully aware of themselves
■ provide a lot of evidence in a short time
■ concentrate on actual behaviour, not reported behaviour.

Downsides
It is true that performance can be limited by the need to 'think on one's feet', but we would not see that as a downside, rather as a demand characteristic of the situation. In addition, some candidates may 'hog' the discussion, limiting others' contributions and opportunities, but again it is up to candidates to act to redress this kind of behaviour.

The greatest threat to validity is that people may be able to 'act' team-orientated and consultative for a short discussion, but may not be that way all the time. However, all assessment requires sampling of behaviour and what you get from a group discussion – which, as noted, is, in principle, considerable – must be triangulated against other evidence which accrues to see if it stands up and can be depended upon.

The worst downside to group discussions – and one that must be given careful thought before using this method – is that it may be harder for some types of candidate to contribute as effectively as others. In practice, this means those in an obvious minority and/or those whose first language is not English.

There are additional pros and cons concerning the choice of assigned role and non-assigned role in group discussions over and above those relating to group discussions in general:

- ■ pros of assigned roles
  - more realistic scenarios
  - allow better assessment of some competencies, e.g. fact-finding, negotiation
  - give a more even chance that everyone has something to contribute
  - easier to diagnose under-performance (poor evidence vs. no evidence).

- ■ pros of non-assigned roles
  - quick and easy to design
  - let a 'natural leader' emerge.

Downsides

An assigned role carries the chore of having to design the roles but it is non-assigned role scenario which has more downsides. Of these, the worst is that candidates can disadvantage themselves by taking on particular roles, for example, scribes find it difficult to contribute fully if they stay as scribes throughout (which they should not do).

New development

Actors can be introduced into group discussions in two ways: first, to provide a focus and context for the group before the actors arrive, and second, once there, the actors can be briefed to shake up the group by requesting to see plans, objectives, etc. Actors can also be briefed to squabble and bicker to find out how adept the group members are at defusing rows and moving the discussion forwards.

Ability tests

Ability tests are standardized tests of reasoning skills using verbal, numerical, or abstract content. Tests usually last between 15 and 45 minutes and are administered under strictly controlled conditions.

Requirements
Test administrators and interpreters must possess the accepted qualification which is British Psychological Society (BPS) Level A.

Advantages
Ability tests have the advantage in that they are relatively pure and objective measures of specific abilities. In addition, they can be administered in groups, and can be linked to comparison groups.

Downsides
It is true that tests can be intimidating, especially for older candidates, but efforts can, and should, be made to relax candidates by sending out familiarization material beforehand and by putting candidates at their ease when they turn up to be tested. Other apparent downsides are:

- Tests may not always appear job-relevant to candidates but a little explanation can put that right.
- Tests require extensive validation. It is not always clear from the product literature that test publishers have validated as much as they should.
- Tests can add a time-pressure element which may not be reflected in the job (although, increasingly, this cannot be true).
- Tests can be influenced by test-taking strategies (although the ability to navigate deftly through a test – what is called 'test-wiseness' – is actually necessary).

New developments
There are no new developments in this method – ability testing has essentially fossilized.

Knowledge or work-sample tests

Knowledge or work-sample tests are timed tests which assess the candidate's knowledge of and dexterity in a specific job-related area.

Advantages
Work-sample tests can be tailored to particular jobs, enabling objective assessment of the level of training experience.

Downsides
The problem with knowledge or work-sample tests is that they:

- can be difficult to standardize
- can be time-consuming to develop, validate and standardize
- may be unfair to certain candidate-groups
- may underplay the candidate's ability to learn, and overplay having a good initial knowledge of the job
- need to be continually updated
- require strict security of materials.

New developments
Commercial products are appearing on the market, notably the 'ABLE' series marketed by Oxford Psychologists Press. However, the variety of tasks and situations is very limited. It would take many tests of this nature before the spectrum of job-related situations could be said to be fully covered. But check for yourself.

Personality questionnaires

Personality questionnaires consist of a set of questions or statements about feelings or behaviour to which individuals must respond. Questionnaires usually ask for preferences – for example, would you prefer bungee jumping or watching TV?

Requirements
Personality test administrators and interpreters must be trained to BPS Level B.

Advantages
Personality questionnaires have the advantages that they are:

- generally reliable and valid
- comprehensive in that they cover all of the basic dimensions of personality
- produce numerical information so that individuals can be more easily compared on the same criteria

■ in principle, a source of good insights into the influence, values and drives of the individual.

Downsides
Being self-reporting, all tests are fakeable – people who want to describe themselves in a positive light can do so. They do not measure how someone is likely to perform in the job (unlike ability tests which can do in part); rather, they measure an individual's preference for behaving in particular ways. For these reasons, the results of personality questionnaires should never be used directly to make a selection decision.

New developments
The only developments are tidying round the edges of Big Five assessment (Big Five being the posited basic dimensions of personality – Extroversion, Neuroticism, Openness, Agreeableness and Conscientiousness). The next new developments are likely to derive from observation of people in real situations or, at least, simulations.

Analysis/presentation exercises

Candidates are given a description of a business problem. They are required to analyse situations and data, and consider alternatives. Candidates may be asked to write a short report, and to give a presentation of their findings to assessors, which will include a question-and-answer session.

Requirements
Assessors need to have well-developed observation and querying skills.

Advantages

■ permit a thorough exploration of analytic and decision-making processes
■ enable the candidate to be observed in action
■ can be made quite realistic and relevant, especially for specialist functions.

Downsides
Poor presentation skills or nervousness can mask good analysis skills if a written report is not assessed (but those sources of interference are themselves evidence).

Case studies

A case study is a realistic and relevant business problem. Candidates must analyse the situation, interpret data, consider alternatives and produce a written report describing their solutions or recommendations.

Advantages
Case studies have the advantages that they:

- provide a reasonably direct measure of relevant skills
- are convenient to administer – can be done in groups
- are easy to interpret – detailed performance indicators can be provided
- are relatively easy to construct and customize
- allow candidates to be directed to answer specific questions in the report.

Downsides
Case studies require care to ensure that the information given to candidates who have direct experience of the situation are not favoured over those who do not (but, again, you would be surprised how many candidates are unable to capitalize on apparent advantage). Up to now, case studies have utilized the handwritten format and, of course, some candidates will have poor writing skills which limit their performance (but again this is evidence, at least, of intellectual grip).

New developments
In future, candidates will write their answers on screen but, needless to say, this will not disguise poor composition skills.

In-tray exercises

Candidates are given a pack of material typical of that found in a manager's in-tray. They have a certain amount of time to deal with the in-tray. Performance can be assessed by interview, and/or by means of a detailed scoring procedure.

Requirements
In-tray exercises require highly skilled assessors/scorers.

Advantages
In-tray exercises have the advantages that they:

- are quite realistic and representative of managerial tasks
- produce a sample of behaviour over a range of tasks

■ provide evidence on a range of competencies
■ can be linked to other activities, for example, future (or past) role-plays, telephone conversations, group discussions.

Downsides
Under-performance in one competency can affect performance in others, for example, poor planning and prioritizing can lead to inappropriate actions later on. Also they may require complicated scoring procedures and can be time-consuming to mark and assess. Perhaps they are more suitable for higher-level management.

New development
Electronic in-trays are catching on, reflecting the daily experience in the workplace, which is based on electronic rather than written communication.

Fact-finding exercises

A fact-finding exercise is a specific type of role-play exercise. Candidates are given an incomplete description of a situation. They must first plan what further information they need, and then carry out an interview with 'an expert' in order to get that information. The candidate then analyses this information, draws conclusions, and presents a set of recommendations to an assessor.

Requirements
Fact-finding exercises require skilled role-players and assessors. Successful and informative exercises depend on role-players responding consistently to all candidates.

Advantages
Fact-finding exercises provide a direct measure of skills which can be difficult to assess in other ways. They also provide an opportunity to explore analysis and reasoning in depth.

Downsides
The resource person supplying the information may hand over or withhold information when not appropriate, but, as always, role-players need careful briefing.

Structured interviews

Structured interviews are made up of separate sections. Each section provides a structured approach to exploring an individual's experience and achievements in a specific area of competence. In practice, a maximum of six sections would be included in an interview.

Requirements
Structured interviews require trained and skilled assessors, as the interviews can be misleading in unskilled hands.

Advantages
Structured interviews have the advantages that they:

- allow for questions to be tailored to an individual's experience
- are focused on behaviour, and derived from detailed competency specifications which are more objective and reliable than conventional interviews
- are easily designed around the competencies
- require little administration or resources
- elicit evidence on a wide number of competencies, and tap a broad range of experience
- provide human contact on a face-to-face and two-way basis
- provide information on several elements that make up any particular competency
- afford the interviewee an opportunity to focus on real events and experiences.

Downsides
With so many advantages, the downsides would need to be considerable to cast doubt on the wisdom of using structured interviews. One we could mention is that the candidate's performance can depend on past performance and experience; those with potential but limited experience may not perform as well. Performance can also be adversely affected by candidates' ability to provide examples. Not everyone has a fund of examples or can bring them to bear when needed. It is also true that a candidate's ability for self-analysis and expression can become key (but that again is evidence, providing assessors are not taken in by the 'gift of the gab').

New developments
Telephone interviews are enjoying a bit of a vogue. With such obvious savings in time this method looks like a winner for streamlined screening. Beware, however, the problems you would expect are indeed problems – absence of body language, lack of non-verbal cues, lapses of silence. Remarked on, too, by those who have been on the receiving end is the prevailing one-way nature of the communication so that it becomes more and more difficult to elicit information on the company. It is as if screen-

ing is really at the uppermost of the interviewers' minds, and not a two-way exchange of information. In terms of fairness, a good piece of advice would be to use telephone interviews for all candidates, or none.

Using methods in combination

Those are the assessment methods considered singly, but assessment methods are used in combination. When weighing up which combination to use it is helpful to think in terms of a theme or themes running through the assessment centre. Candidates are thankful not to have to adjust to a new fictitious scenario, so, for example, let the same company names and personalities run through the various exercises. Explicitly link one exercise to another, for example, something in an in-tray can lead to a role-play and to a group exercise. Something in a group-orientated case study can lead to an individual one-to-one exercise. But make sure that success in a linked exercise is not dependent on success or failure in a previous exercise. That is not fair.

Matching exercises to competencies

Evidently, some exercises are more suited to tapping certain competencies than others. You will not get at 'leadership' with a written case study or at 'analysis' with a group discussion. Table 6.1 provides a checklist for choosing the exercises most appropriate for assessing particular competencies. It also conveys the range and type of exercises most commonly used.

The salience of graduate perceptions

We reported in Chapter 3 that graduates, in general, find interviews, work samples and ability tests to be the most fair and relevant assessment methods. All very interesting, you may say, but why, as an employer, should I take any notice? The answer is that graduates are likely to tell their friends about the assessment process; what a graduate hears about an organization's processes is likely to affect whether they themselves apply to that organization.

Above all, the image an organization projects in relation to its application and selection process may influence an applicant's decision to accept an offer. Graduates may like interviews but they are unlikely to be impressed at being asked to attend three or more interviews (it happens). Organizations that do this are only conveying indecision.

Table 6.1   A checklist for choosing exercises most appropriate for assessing particular competencies, and those most commonly used

	IN-TRAY & DEBRIEF	GROUP DISCUSSION (ASSIGNED ROLES)	GROUP DISCUSSION (NON-ASSIGNED ROLES)	CASE STUDY	INTERVIEW	FACT-FINDING	ROLE-PLAY	ORAL PRESENTATION
Time to mark (mins): 1 competency Whole exercise	20 60	15 45	15 45	20 60	10 40	10 40	15 45	10 45
COMPETENCIES								
ACHIEVEMENT								
Initiative/Proactivity ■ does not wait to be told what to do ■ instigates action to achieve objectives	✓✓	✓✓	✓✓		✓✓		✓	
Work standards ■ identifies better ways of doing things ■ regularly meets standards set	✓✓		✓✓	✓	✓✓			

Planning & organizing ■ develops detailed action plans ■ determines priorities for tasks	✓✓		✓	✓✓		
Tenacity ■ perseveres when progress blocked ■ follows issues through to conclusion	✓✓			✓✓	✓✓	✓
Independence ■ stands up for own decisions ■ takes responsibility for results	✓✓			✓✓	✓	✓
Adaptability ■ thinks on feet during discussions with staff ■ understands the need for change				✓✓		

Continued

85

MANAGEMENT BEHAVIOUR	IN-TRAY & DEBRIEF	GROUP DISCUSSION (ASSIGNED ROLES)	GROUP DISCUSSION (NON-ASSIGNED ROLES)	CASE STUDY	INTERVIEW	FACT-FINDING	ROLE-PLAY	ORAL PRESENTATION
Delegation ■ identifies opportunities for delegation ■ supports others after delegation	✓✓				✓✓		✓	
Monitoring & controlling ■ sets measurable goals ■ reviews progress against set goals	✓✓				✓✓		✓✓	
Developing others ■ identifies and supports individual strengths ■ demonstrates belief that others want to learn	✓				✓✓		✓	
Leadership ■ communicates enthusiasm to others ■ explains reasons for action		✓✓	✓✓		✓✓		✓✓	

Team work ■ shares ideas and information ■ supports fellow team members		✓✓		✓✓		
ANALYTICAL THINKING						
Risk taking ■ Prepared to take calculated risks ■ takes decisions in times of uncertainty	✓✓	✓		✓✓	✓✓	✓✓
Analysis ■ identifies key issues from information ■ identifies logical flaws in information	✓✓	✓		✓✓	✓✓	✓✓
Judgement ■ considers consequences of decisions ■ evaluates several opinions	✓✓	✓		✓✓	✓✓	✓✓

Continued

87

ANALYTICAL THINKING cont'd	IN-TRAY & DEBRIEF	GROUP DISCUSSION (ASSIGNED ROLES)	GROUP DISCUSSION (NON-ASSIGNED ROLES)	CASE STUDY	INTERVIEW	FACT-FINDING	ROLE-PLAY	ORAL PRESENTATION
Decisiveness ■ relates decisions to work priorities ■ knows when to take a decision	✓✓		✓	✓✓	✓	✓✓	✓✓	✓✓
Creativity ■ suggests new ideas ■ approaches problems from novel angles				✓	✓✓			
Strategic thinking ■ looks for long-term implications ■ sees the bigger picture	✓✓		✓✓	✓✓	✓✓			
Information seeking ■ uses several sources to gain information ■ consults widely before decision making		✓✓				✓		

IMPACT

Impact								
■ uses evidence to support arguments	✓✓	✓✓		✓✓			✓✓	✓✓
■ presents self smartly and professionally								
Oral communication	✓✓	✓✓		✓✓			✓✓	✓✓
■ speaks clearly								
■ does not make assumptions								
Oral presentation	✓✓	✓✓			✓			✓✓
■ tailors talk to audience								
■ makes appropriate use of visual aids								
Written communication	✓✓				✓✓			
■ communicates concisely								
■ communicates legibly								
Persuasiveness	✓✓	✓✓		✓✓	✓✓	✓✓	✓	✓✓
■ presents arguments rationally								
■ actively 'sells' ideas								

Continued

IMPACT cont'd	IN-TRAY & DEBRIEF	GROUP DISCUSSION (ASSIGNED ROLES)	GROUP DISCUSSION (NON-ASSIGNED ROLES)	CASE STUDY	INTERVIEW	FACT-FINDING	ROLE-PLAY	ORAL PRESENTATION
Organizational sensitivity ■ develops and maintains a wide network of contacts ■ has a cross-functional perspective	✓			✓	✓✓		✓	✓
Sensitivity ■ shows respect and fairness to people ■ hears the concerns of others	✓✓	✓✓	✓✓				✓✓	
PERSONAL EFFECTIVENESS								
Self-confidence ■ challenges the status quo ■ does not take criticism personally		✓✓	✓✓		✓✓	✓✓	✓✓	✓✓

Key: ✓✓ Competency observed over 90% of the time
✓ Competency observed over 90% of the time in certain exercises in this category, but not all

Behavioural flexibility ▪ handles many issues simultaneously ▪ adapts style to different situations		✓✓					✓✓
Organizational commitment ▪ is consistent with company values ▪ aligns activities and organizational goals		✓✓		✓✓	✓✓	✓✓	✓✓
Stress tolerance/ resilience ▪ keeps emotions under control ▪ demonstrates stamina		✓✓	✓✓	✓	✓		✓✓
OTHER							
Technical knowledge & business understanding	✓✓			✓✓	✓	✓✓	✓✓
Customer focus				✓✓	✓✓		✓✓
Continuous improvement				✓✓		✓✓	✓✓
Sales ability	✓✓	✓✓		✓✓	✓✓		✓✓

Concluded

It is worth making every effort to explain to candidates the reason for using particular assessment methods (regardless of whether candidates perceive them to be fair/relevant). Explain clearly what skills you are trying to assess during particular exercises, and try to obtain feedback from candidates on what you have done. If possible, include one or more of the assessment methods that graduates find relevant and fair. Since one is the interview – which is universal – that should not be difficult.

Key points from this chapter

- Organizations need to be specific in the competencies against which they wish to assess graduates. These competencies should be *recruitment-relevant*. They are the competencies that are required to perform the job *immediately*.
- All assessment methods have advantages and downsides. Some duplicate each other to an extent; some – like the interview – do a job the others cannot. A recruitment process should combine assessment methods in such a way as to maximize validity and utility.
- What the applicants themselves think comes into consideration of utility. It is only being pragmatic to take note of what they like and don't like. If possible, include one or more of the assessment methods that graduates find relevant and fair. Since one is the interview – which is universal – that should not be difficult.

The global graduate recruiter

Increasingly, multinational companies and organizations see themselves as global entities, employing a global workforce situated entirely in the private sector. There is, of course, no such thing as a global public sector.

Companies that have substantial interests outside the parent country include nearly all the world's 500 largest organizations. For example, 39 per cent of the Ford Motor Company's employees work outside the United States and 43 per cent of ICI's employees work outside the United Kingdom. Unilever, Royal Dutch/Shell Group and IBM all boast international teams, and there are many more.

As a consequence, the mind-set towards employees is starting to change. In the past, typically, the most senior positions, at home and abroad, would be occupied by nationals of the home country. Away from the home country, senior positions would be occupied by expatriates, with the nationals of the non-home country progressing up to a certain point but not beyond. Now, it is increasingly the case that organizations are viewing the whole of the workforce as a corporate global resource to be used throughout the world. This development is bound to impact on graduate recruitment, and already is. 'Go global' says Carlsberg-Tetley in a 1999 advertisement. The advertisement was for international trainees, eight months in the UK followed by 16 months in Copenhagen. 'After successful completion', the advert says, 'you'll be ready to take key positions with either Carlsberg-Tetley or any other international Carlsberg company.'

Of course, companies are assisted and encouraged in their global plans by the willingness of an increasing number of students to work internationally. Foreign travel has increased, the teaching of foreign languages has improved, and the cost of international travel has come down considerably. Consequently, there are increasing numbers of people who think beyond their national boundaries, and who have experience of other countries and cultures.

With the expansion of global trade and free-trade zones, there is increasing freedom of movement of goods and services, as well as of labour, across countries. The global graduate recruiter is likely to see graduates as a potential corporate resource providing the organization with a cadre of people who can move around the world easily, settle in quickly, and communicate well. Companies are looking for people who not only have the intellectual capacity to tackle business issues but who also appreciate diversity and who, in addition, are fluent in at least two languages. Such people are likely to be relatively rare and will be rarer still if the search for them is restricted to only one country.

But if graduates are to be seen as a potential global resource to be selected in different locations throughout the world, then a major issue becomes how to set standards to ensure, as far as possible, that people of comparable quality are being picked from each country. An important part of any strategy, therefore, will be the establishment of corporate standards which are agreed for all parts of the organization.

While on the surface this may appear a daunting task, in practice it can be achieved, given time, patience, and a commitment to keep all parties involved in the process. The example below illustrates how this was achieved in a fast- moving consumer goods organization.

Developing competencies within a fast-moving consumer goods organization

The objective in this organization, based in north-western Europe, was to establish common criteria for accountants and financial controllers around the world. The primary reason for developing these new criteria was that these roles had changed considerably in recent years from one of policing and monitoring finances to one of providing financial advice to all parts of the business and being active participants in the decision-making process. It was felt that people would be able to make these changes more easily if they knew clearly what was expected of them.

A group of financial directors was created to act as a focus group and a sounding board for the project. The selection process ensured that all parts of the business in all parts of the globe were represented – a genuinely multinational team. The team was interviewed beforehand and briefed as to what the project was about; they were also given papers which were relevant to their tasks, for example, notes from meetings that had taken place to discuss the new role, frameworks that had been developed else-where. The group met in Europe and over two days they identified the necessary role-changes and moved on to produce a competency framework. This has been refined by consulting a wider range of groups and has been used not only to develop existing controllers but as a basis for graduate recruitment globally. Their initial discussions were based on critical inci-dents, which were then broken down into behavioural statements, and these statements were then categorized into similar groups of behaviour. A process of examining, reviewing and refining the behavioural statements eventually whittled the competencies down to twelve.

At the end of the two days these twelve sets of competencies and indica-tors were typed up, reviewed again by psychologists involved in the project, and a few weeks later a second meeting held to review the revised com-petencies. Further refinements were made and then the competencies sent out for wider discussion around the world.

As this was an international project, it was important that members cooperated with one another and listened to what people were saying about cultural differences and how these would be applied to the behavioural indicators. A wider discussion with people beyond this group also took place and that feedback was incorporated. These competencies were obviously applicable to people joining the role on a global basis, but also they were to be used as a basis for global graduate recruitment.

For graduate recruitment, the competencies have been modified so that they are relevant to be used with relatively inexperienced students. At this stage, each operating company uses its own selection methods, but the competencies enable the organization to attain consistency in the qualities it is seeking from its finance graduates. The next step currently being planned is to run European-wide assessment centres which aim to intro-duce consistency in the company's assessment techniques.

If people are expected to work internationally, then some sensitivity to diversity and the ability to adapt when posted to different countries are essential; such competencies need to be included in any competency framework.

Once the criteria have been established it is likely that some local flexibility is going to be required. At a general level, in our experience, the competency headings will probably not change much from one culture to another. However, it is likely that some of the indicators may change, particularly for those competencies which relate to communication and interpersonal skills. In China, a competency called the Relations Competency (RC) is reckoned to be essential for successful leadership. In Thailand, quietness and modesty are esteemed. If you are recruiting for China and/or Thailand you need to know such things.

Global recruitment campaigns

If an organization is to engage in global graduate recruitment, campaigns should be co-ordinated strategically but with regional variations and differences. These differences will be in response to local market con-ditions and expectations, for example, differences in educational systems, local perceptions, and images of the organization.

As all candidates are going to be assessed against the same competen-cies, the graduate recruitment literature needs to reflect the competencies that are being sought. These are messages that can be transmitted across the world to all potential applicants.

Decisions also need to be made about how widespread the trawl for suitable students should be. In some countries it is common for students to travel abroad to obtain further education. It is common for students from Southeast Asia and Africa to study at universities in Europe and the US. It follows that organizations seeking graduates to work initially in the Indian sub-continent, Southeast Asia and Africa, would need to think about extending their graduate recruitment drives to include the UK and the US in order for these expatriate students to be considered for selection.

Multilateral recruitment evidently requires global coordination if it is to run smoothly. One organization we know runs an Asian Forum in the United States where expatriate students from Asia can apply. HR managers from the relevant Asian countries then come to the US to assess these students and their suitability for the roles advertised.

Developing global selection processes

Cultural differences will have an impact on global selection. The research shows that there are some key ways in which cultures differ. For selection processes some of the most important differences will be around:

- the universalism–particularism dimension
- the extent to which people show their emotions
- communication and interpersonal styles.

The universalism–particularism dimension refers to the extent to which rules are seen to apply to everyone and to the degree of flexibility that is allowed. For example, the UK and Sweden (though they are not alone) are reckoned to be universalist cultures, where a set of rules will be applied in more or less the same way to everyone.

In a particularist culture, by contrast, it is the nature of the relationship that you have with someone which will determine how you will react to him or her. If you know someone particularly well and feel confident in the relationship you might show more flexibility towards them, you might even reward them with a job.

In Europe, France would be regarded as having a particularist society; elsewhere, Japan is considered to have a particularly strong particularist orientation. The drive always is towards customizing goods so as to please the individual. But the tendency to treat individual customers with extreme consideration can lead to scandal, as when Japanese brokerage houses voluntarily repay the losses of their favourite customers with money that has come from the less favoured. Corruption typically takes the form of doing too much for special individuals.

So a response or gesture that might be considered acceptable in Japan is liable to be considered unacceptable in Sweden. It is easy to imagine how these potent societal forces could have an impact on graduate selection processes, especially case studies, in-tray exercises and other problem-solving activities.

The importance of family can also have an impact. For example, it has been said that techniques such as competency-based interviewing will not work in Asian countries because people there do not want to talk about their achievements. Our experience running development centres in Malaysia, Thailand, Singapore and the Philippines has not borne this out.

Asian students seem as comfortable as Western students in describing events that have happened to them. There is a caveat, however. You must be prepared for different types of examples. For example, when interviewing in Singapore, local students were more likely than British students to give examples which were connected with their families. When asked to give an example of persuading or influencing someone to her point of view, a female student gave the example of explaining to her parents why she preferred another university to the one they had hoped she would go to. The assessors, all Singaporean, agreed this was a good example. Assessors from the UK felt that without knowledge of the importance placed on family they would not have rated this so highly.

This example highlights the importance of using an international group of assessors – people who can apply the competencies and selection processes locally. It is unlikely that organizations will be effective if they simply try to replicate their home-based operations abroad.

To ignore the real cultural differences and influences that come into play when important decisions are made could result in someone very able being rejected because the context in which they live and work is not properly appreciated by those making the assessments.

There are, of course, differences in the extent to which people from different cultures show their emotions. One study found that, in a rank order of countries, the Japanese were least likely to show their emotions, with Italians most likely to. If you are looking for communication skills and the ability to engage other people, this display of emotion may be misunderstood in what are superficially the same contexts.

Also to be taken into consideration is the extent to which people are prepared to speak up in groups and to push themselves forward. For example, a Japanese manager working for a US company in Tokyo told us that he acts far more modestly and quietly when in Japanese groups than when in mixed or predominantly American groups (and indeed we observed him doing so). He had learned that to be effective in different settings it was necessary for him to understand and to adapt to the different expectations people had of one another.

On the question of interpersonal styles there are other issues, such as strength of expression when speaking, the extent to which people talk across one another, how close people stand to each other, even the extent of eye contact. All of these factors can impact on assessment processes, and unless we are aware of them we may make poor decisions. Consequently, a selection process that is developed within one culture, and which is reliable and valid within that culture, may become less reliable and less valid once used on a multinational group of applicants.

An example of what we are talking about would be the use of personality questionnaires or 360-degree appraisal instruments. The tendency of raters in different countries to give more lenient or severe ratings has been documented. Knowing this, you, as a results interpreter, must adjust broadly depending on where you are (although, of course, the relativities still carry meaningful information).

Feedback to participants following a development or assessment centre is another area where you need to be watchful. Here you have to confront the possibility of cultural differences in the way participants are going to receive feedback. To motivate the discussion, consider the concept of human nature. It has been suggested that if people in a culture conceive human beings as essentially good, negative traits are seen as unimportant (since they don't provide information about what that person is really like) whereas positive traits are seen as important (because they do provide information as to what the person is really like). If, however, people in a culture believe that human beings may be good and/or bad, both positive and negative traits would be seen as important because they are both 'diagnostic' of what people are really like.

The last position corresponds, by and large, to the world view that informs the way we (the authors) give feedback on performance. We praise the strengths (and, if applicable, talk about how they could be used to work on weaknesses), and then we talk about the weaknesses and what can be done to rectify them. Of course, we recognize that most people like to hear about their strengths and hate to hear about their shortcomings, although few have gone as far as Trompenaar's African who shot the bringer of what he saw as negative feedback (don't kill the messenger). That said, having set up the discussion around strengths, it is usually possible to introduce weaknesses (the euphemism is 'development needs' or 'areas for improvement') and to give them an airing.

From time to time, however, we encounter situations or people where it becomes plain that weaknesses are not on the agenda. An example would be a Singaporean who attended a development centre in Australia. He is (was) an internal auditor who prided himself on his professional integrity, his expertise, and his drive and commitment to the company. But he did not want to stay an auditor; he wanted to become first a chief financial officer and then a general manager. However, in order to qualify for either of these jobs he had been told that he needed to work on his interpersonal skills, especially influencing upwards – the word used was 'diplomacy'.

The development centre confirmed this to be the case and also pointed to some other interpersonal things he might work on. The strengths were mentioned but we said we could not confirm them because we had not seen them at the development centre (this man was very quiet).

When the summary report was circulated there was consternation, as in: this man is a top internal auditor recognized as such by his colleagues: why does your report not say this? We do not recognize this man you are writing about.'

Was this an instance of only what is positive is important? And what is negative doesn't matter because it isn't informative? But it was informative – by common consent, the man needed to work on communicating appropriately with his bosses. Certainly what was positive was important, for his professional self-esteem was threatened. But he had forgotten that he did not want (so he said) to be the best internal auditor in the world, he wanted to be something else (perhaps in Europe) and to be that something else he had to change.

The fact is that feedback cannot be all about strengths whatever the assessors imagine is prized in that culture. Otherwise what is the point of a development centre and how, in the context of global deployment where employees must operate in more or less Western work environments, can companies ignore weaknesses? But there are different ways of getting across messages, and local assessors and observers ought to be able to advise on how best to couch the messages – what buttons to press – so as to get the best results.

Adapting selection processes

What can be done to adapt home-based selection processes to work in these changed circumstances? There are a number of strategies:

- First of all, check the language content of the materials being used in selection. Is the level of English required to do a test or exercise higher than that needed to carry out the work? Are colloquialisms and unnecessary jargon being used? If this is the case then you may be building in a disadvantage for people whose first language is not English.
- Where organizations are attempting to take stock of the people with senior management potential or seeking to recruit from different countries, then the first stage at least should be carried out locally. This could include translating tests and other exercises, and allowing interviews to be carried out in the candidate's first language. Obviously, however, some assessment will need to be made of their level of written and spoken English.
- Particular care needs to be taken about group processes. Assessors need to be carefully trained. But over and above that you should be wary of using these exercises too much. Cultural differences will probably be more apparent in these than in any other form of assessment.
- Generally speaking, the competencies which organizations develop tend to be appropriate globally. However, the indicators may need reviewing, as some approaches to issues may differ from culture to culture. However, one competency that needs to be included is something related to cultural diversity and the extent to which applicants show sensitivity to this.

■ Better preparation of candidates will help them become aware of what will happen. Giving them details about what will take place – making the process transparent – is important. Also more time should be allowed for practice and indeed even coaching.

■ All exercises, competencies, indicators, etc. should be developed in conjunction with a multinational team. This will reduce the possibility of ending up with a very biased process.

■ A source of information not to be overlooked will be the experiences of the candidates themselves. Together with monitoring of the outcomes these data can be used to revise the process in the future.

■ Check out the suitability of any personality questionnaires proposed for use.

■ When evidence is being discussed and synthesized at the end (the 'wash-up'), talk about what a suitable approach to report writing and feedback would be. There are two aspects to this – what is to be said face to face, and what is to be written as a record. To find out what are the buttons to press for each individual, ask the locals.

Key points from this chapter

■ The number of people who think beyond their national boundaries, and who have experience of other countries and cultures, is increasing.

■ If people are expected to work internationally then some sensitivity to diversity and the ability to adapt are essential; such competencies need to be included in any competency framework.

■ Cultural differences will have an impact on global selection. Important differences will be around treating everyone the same vs. favouring some, the extent to which people show their emotions, and communication and interpersonal styles.

■ When formulating recruitment schemes, the importance of consulting people from different cultures cannot be overestimated. It is unlikely that organizations will recruit effectively if they do no more than replicate their home-based operations abroad.

■ Practical steps can be taken to adapt home-based selection processes to work in these changed circumstances, for example, check the language content of the materials being used in selection and avoid over-reliance on group exercises. Cultural differences will probably be more apparent in these than in any other form of assessment.

Recruiting graduate high flyers

In looking for high flyers, organizations are looking for people with the potential to progress to more senior levels within the organization. It follows that a more targeted approach to selection would appear to be needed in order to pinpoint those people who have the capability to make rapid progress through the organization. Identification of potential, however, is difficult, particularly with people who may have very little relevant work experience. It is made even more difficult if – as we believe – what constitutes potential is not as straightforward as would appear on the surface. A conventional formulation in terms of, say, brains plus charisma (whatever that is) may not do.

Some organizations use high potential or fast-track or fast-stream programmes to progress the high flyers; others prefer not to, and may not group the high flyers together or even label them as such. There is some point in not labelling. The very existence of fast-track programmes sends out signals and generates expectations, not always predictable or desirable. It is obvious that if not managed effectively and reviewed regularly, the morale and productivity of those who are not on the scheme can be affected negatively, with knock-on effects for those on the scheme.

The promise of joining a fast-track programme is, of course, an inducement to applicants. It is certainly part of the recruitment message. To produce future leaders might be the overt purpose of the programme but the real agenda for the organization might have more to do with expediency: to make sure we get our fair share (or even more than our fair share) of the best graduates, whatever 'best' means. To say that fast tracks function as honeypots to attract new and recent graduates may not be too wide of the mark.

You could go further and say that the less attractive an organization is, the more it needs a fast track. The Civil Service knows that. A 1994 review of its fast-stream operation found that 60 per cent of people on the fast stream would not have applied had there not been one in place.

Then there are organizations with an undeniably down-market image which struggle to attract any talent. A few years ago, Fosters, the high-street menswear retailer, advertised a fast track with the slogan 'Further, Faster, Fosters'. It must have been a desperate last throw of the dice: Fosters went into liquidation soon after.

In this chapter we look at what constitutes potential and how to find those that have it. We also examine fast-track programmes, the positive steps to take and the pitfalls to avoid.

Potential to get to the top – what to look for

In May 2000, a furore was provoked by talk about 'potential'. Even the Chancellor of the Exchequer got involved amid allegations of elitism. The furore concerned a student from a comprehensive in the Northeast who applied to Magdalen College, Oxford to study medicine and was turned down because they 'weren't sure that she had potential'.

Like so many others who bandy the term about, these academics quite missed the point – potential for *what*, exactly? Potential to get a first, potential to become a brain surgeon, potential to become a good GP, a fine medical teacher, what exactly? You can't talk about potential in the generality. Calling people 'high potentials' (as a stylistic alternative to 'high flyers') is meaningless unless you specify it to 'potential to become a senior manager' or some such.

Remember our six types of graduates in Chapter 1? Fast track was the first type. Hiring graduate high flyers is like hiring graduates except that you want the very best. But what is the 'best' given that the potential being looked for is, shall we say, 'potential to become a future Chief Executive'?

To answer this question, ordinarily we would call for an analysis of the qualities being sought. Questions would need to be asked, such as:

- Which graduates have succeeded into senior management?
- How can the good graduate performers be differentiated from the less good?
- What qualities will we want of our future senior management?

Ordinarily, these are the right questions to ask, but beware. Beware trying to reproduce the past. A competency model based on who is successful *now* cannot be relevant to the future where change is certain. A study of international executives found that what differentiated successful high flyers from solid performers was their ability to learn from experience, to adapt in the face of changing circumstances, to acquire new skills when they need them. This has been referred to as the 'capacity to have capacities' (rather than the capacity to perform now) or, if you like, *adaptitude*. It must be part – perhaps the integral part – of what potential is about. We are talking about *learning* competencies.

It comes down to this. When looking for future leaders we cannot rely as much as we would like on typical methodology, that is, analyse successful performance now, call the ingredients X, and then look for X in others. Actually, not X exactly but a scaled-down version of X, fully expecting that with the passage of time little X will become big X. This has been called the 'Russian Doll syndrome'. But corporate life is not like that. Formative experiences cannot be foretold. Things happen. Choices have to be made. The tiniest Russian Doll may not resemble in any way the biggest Doll.

Work done by the Centre for Creative Leadership (CCL) in the US, and confirmed by UK researchers at Oxford Psychologists Press (OPP), identified the three ingredients for successful chief executives:

■ handling the demands of the management job
■ dealing with subordinates
■ having respect for self and others.

In other words, success depends on results *and* relationships, results through people rather than with people, where the results are the 'demands' and the relationships are the dealings with others and self. Going further, some specific qualities were identified, namely resourcefulness, doing whatever it takes, being a quick learner, and decisiveness.

Devotees of the concept of emotional intelligence (EI) will see running through these formulations elements of EI such as persistence, self-awareness, self-control, empathy with others, and flexibility. With the addition of something like drive for results, which is in some ways covered anyway by persistence, potential could easily be conceptualized in terms of EI.

Flying too near the sun

The CCL work also looked at high flyers who failed or derailed. Initially, predictions of success were based on their track record, technical or business competence, outgoing personality, loyalty to management, and willingness to lead. Then they derailed – why? Among the reasons given were declining business performance; having an insensitive, abrasive, intimidating style; being cold, aloof and arrogant; over-managing; being poor at choosing staff, and being overly ambitious.

The reality is that all competencies have their dark sides. The manager earmarked as action-orientated turns out to be reckless and dictatorial; the one who is said to be good with people turns out to be soft, unable to make tough decisions, and poor at choosing staff because afraid of hiring challenging people. The challenge for assessors is to try to spot early signs of derailment risk. Arrogance is usually a tell-tale sign.

Are learning competencies catching on? A glance at the twelve most common competencies, those which emerge time and time again, suggests not:

■ communication
■ achievement/results orientation

- customer focus
- teamwork
- leadership
- planning and organizing
- commercial/business awareness
- flexibility/adaptability
- developing others
- problem solving
- analytical thinking
- building relationships.

Only flexibility/adaptability could be classed as a learning competency, although building relationships is important, too. The rest are *performance* competencies.

What has the Civil Service been looking for in its fast-stream entrants? Here is the list:

1. Penetration
2. Fertility of ideas
3. Judgement
4. Written expression
5. Oral expression
6. Personal contacts
7. Influence
8. Drive
9. Determination
10. Reliability.

Nothing there about learning, although 'drive' and 'determination' would be part of potential. There is, however, a number 11 which looks promising: capacity for development. The instruction for assessors says: 'Using all the information about the candidate, including present strengths and weaknesses, assess him or her on capacity for development.' We doubt very much if assessors could get a good handle on that competency with those instructions.

To summarize, then, for graduate high flyers the *recruitment-relevant competencies* are not so much the performance competencies but learning competencies, such as:

- flexible in dealing with others
- learns from mistakes
- accepts and acts on feedback
- adapts to changing circumstances including cultural diversity.

These competencies would be augmented by attributes like 'builds relationships', 'self-awareness' and 'drives for results'. The outcome is a specification for a selection process which looks very different from the conventional assessment vehicle.

Selecting graduate high flyers

Given the thrust of our argument, it is clear that a different approach is needed from what has been customary. Practically, it means this: if learning competencies are going to be key, then the content of assessment events must change. Assessment must move away from concentration on competencies which are about performance now, like planning and organizing and analytical thinking, towards the future-related competencies. Dynamic exercises will need to be introduced into assessment centres which will allow these competencies to be targeted and assessed directly.

For us, the way through is to regard learning competencies as *second-order* skills to be judged through the assessment of *first-order* skills, which are the performance competencies. Thus a second-order skill such as 'learns from mistakes' can be accessed by asking the candidate to undertake an exercise more than once; similarly, another second-order skill like 'accepts and acts on feedback' can be picked up when observing how candidates react to feedback on their first (and maybe second) attempts. It is obvious how another second-order skill like 'persistence' could be evaluated over the course of a three-day event.

So, elements of such an assessment event based around learning competencies could be:

■ Ongoing feedback by coaches (to get a handle on second-order skills)
■ Repetition of some exercises (in order to see what is learned and get a handle on second-order skills)
■ Self-assessment (what am I learning about myself)
■ Peer assessment (what am I seeing in others that will help me learn about myself).

There is a problem, however, which was already alluded to at the beginning of this chapter. Spotting talent that will endure requires in-depth investigation. It is not enough to base judgements on one assessment centre or a year's good performance. You need to look at different types of evidence to spot any warning signs of derailment. But with new graduates you neither have the time to spend ascertaining potential nor the track record. This means that all too often high flyers are designated as such on the basis of limited personal experience or observations in a pressured, high-visibility, atypical situation.

It is worth remembering, however, that you are not totally dependent on the assessment event for evidence. New graduates do have CVs and can bring forward evidence from their lives on what we are calling learning competencies. Something like 'adapting to changing circumstances' is one where young people could certainly be expected to have positive evidence to submit.

We said earlier that the challenge for assessors is to try to spot early signs of derailment risk. To do so will require a shift in mind-set, because typically we try to accentuate the positive and look for what is good or developable rather than what is liable to prove the candidate's undoing. Personality questionnaires which attempt overtly to probe the 'dark side' – like the California Personality Inventory (CPI) and Hogan – can be useful here, with the proviso already stated that these questionnaires should never be the sole criterion for rejecting candidates.

In terms of administration, candidates will need to feel that they have been specially chosen and that being part of the selection process is a success in itself. The number of participants at each event needs to be kept small, but the organization needs to be confident of the quality of the people attending them. The number of assessors and support staff needs to be increased so that each candidate is handled by an assigned administrator whose job it is to keep the candidate informed of what is happening. Evidently, more time will be required than usual and more assessors will be needed. These events are bound to be resource-intensive but then the stakes are high.

High-potential or fast-track programmes

Critical factors associated with high-potential or fast-track programmes include:

■ effective career management
■ levels of responsibility
■ job rotations
■ high-profile support
■ dynamic nature of the programme
■ managing people not on the programme.

Effective career management
Research to date, and our own experience, indicates that the one vital key to success is the provision of effective career management after the ending of any formal programme. Motivation and direction are easily maintained in the controlled environment of a fast-track programme but maintenance becomes much harder once the individual leaves the programme – it is here that the organization must strive to accommodate the sophisticated career aspirations of its high-achieving employees.

The calibre of top management is one of the few ways companies can get an edge over the competition. The retention of high-calibre senior management needs to be built into any programme of high-potential development, given the importance of this group to the strategic success of the company.

Research has shown that where obligations which form the psychological contract are reasonably met, the majority of employees will maintain high levels of commitment to the organization. This can still be the case where obligations are unmet, as long as the employee perceives that there has been reasonable effort to meet these obligations. It follows that organizations need to give thought to putting in place effective career management processes to identify regularly what the needs and motivations of the individuals are and to ensure that these can be reasonably met.

Thomson, the French multinational, suffered for many years from high attrition rates among its high-potential employees. A familiar situation developed. As these people became highly skilled they also became extremely marketable. To tackle the high level of departures, Thomson devised a concept called a 'Development Convention', which participants of all its fast-track programmes attend. The Development Convention is a week-long event where high flyers meet and interface with senior management, and engage in various activities and seminars designed to communicate to them their value to the company. The idea is that such an event engenders a sense of loyalty and understanding of the strategic aims of the organization and the part that high-flying employees can play in achieving the organization's goals.

Responsibility

Challenging levels of responsibility are also key factors in the retention of high achievers (according to research undertaken by the Management School at Ashridge). The perception held by high-potential employees is that responsibility and challenging work are the most important factors in improving their employability. They see employability as determining their success in the future, as many have adjusted to the fact that there is no job for life.

The nature and intensity of the projects which high-potential individuals are given to work on are critical if the programme is to be perceived as successful. The very nature of being on a high-potential programme suggests that the type of individuals who join seek challenging work with reasonable levels of responsibility. The ability to make a difference to the organization which can engender a sense of value is important if psychological contracts are to be kept strong and job satisfaction levels kept high.

Flat organizational structures may pose a particular problem, as there is evidence that flattened structures more or less neutralize high flyers and their ambitions. All that happens to erstwhile high potentials is that they do more work and do not move upwards. A Roffey Park report claims that one in four high flyers in the UK are 'jumping ship'. Yet as organizations reinstate hierarchy and fast tracks, they run the risk of alienating staff not considered to be high flyers.

Job rotations

Managing job rotations successfully is key. Timing is crucial. An individual must be given sufficient time to engage in a project at a deep enough level to be satisfying, but not too long that the individual loses motivation and a sense of direction in fulfilling their wider goals.

Job rotations can fail due to a negative prevailing culture. Managers may not wish to give high-potential employees challenging projects for fear of being outshone, as well as not wishing to allow the individual to become involved in an intensive project that will last longer than the duration of the individual's time in a department.

High-profile support

Success of high-potential programmes has been strongly linked to high-profile support for and presence within the scheme. In the past, British Airways, for example, ensured that a percentage of each year's High Flyers become Personal Assistants to the Chief Executive in the middle year of their programmes. The idea is that they have direct access to the strategic power base, and are thus able to obtain a sense of the overall strategic aims of the airline. Managers of the scheme then foster intensive networking among high-potential employees to enable those with this experience to communicate both formally and informally their experiences and insights to their peers.

Lack of support may materialize where the high flyer is perceived as not fitting into the culture of the organization. Innovation and creativity may be valued but it can be the very talent that others fear. A system of coaches and/or mentors needs to be established so that high potentials always have some support within the organization.

Dynamic nature of the programme

For any scheme to succeed it must be dynamic. Research shows that schemes which encourage feedback and monitoring of its effectiveness at regular intervals, and then allow modification, are more successful in retaining high-potential employees than those that do not, or do not do it enough. For example, Microsoft has managed to keep its key staff for many years. Surveys are carried out regularly to find out what would continue to keep these key staff motivated. By listening and responding, where there is a business case, to what these individuals want, Microsoft is able to maintain and even build on existing loyalty.

It appears that high-potential employees seek motivating and challenging work more than financial reward, especially when related to performance. Research by IDS, the pay analysis firm, has shown that paying above-average salaries to high-potential employees in the beginning results in greater loyalty later on. IDS found that of the organizations which paid their high flyers above-average starting salaries, 67 per cent were still with the same employer five years later. What is perhaps surprising is that performance-related pay for these high flyers was not a strong motivator.

Managing people outside the fast-track programme
The problem – and it is a big problem – is that people not on the programme will have aspirations and development needs equal to, if not greater than, those on the programme. In any organization there will be people – perhaps many people – who have the potential to progress further if identified soon enough and treated seriously and constructively. If ability to learn from experience, from failure, is key, why imagine that it is to be found only among the brainy and the charismatic? The CCL suggests conducting regular talent searches throughout the whole organization, encouraging nominations from staff, and putting in place reviewers whose job it is to look for talent.

Key points from this chapter

- Loose talk about potential helps no one. The concept needs to be closely defined to be of value.
- The capacity to adapt to changing circumstances and to learn from mistakes is likely to be the factor which separates the top achievers from the rest.
- Conventionally conceived assessment events will not do the job in this new dispensation. Attention should be given to introducing more dynamic into events so that particular skills, such as accepting and acting on feedback, can be observed. Attention should also be given to early identification of risk of derailment later on.
- High-potential or fast-track programmes can easily unravel if neglected or taken for granted. The very existence of fast-track programmes sends out signals and generates expectations, not always predictable or desirable. It is also dangerous to suppose that all future top management will come from these schemes.
- Finally, let us not forget middle and low flyers. Charles Handy, for one, has been at pains to point out how any organization absolutely needs some average workers ('followers'), just as you need adapters as well as innovators. And they all need development.

After recruitment: why induction matters

This chapter is about induction – much talked about, less often practised, or at least practised properly. But what is proper induction, anyway? We try to provide an answer. We also use our own sponsored research to talk about current practices used to induct graduates and what graduates themselves think of induction they have experienced.

Inducting graduates

The key challenge facing graduates on entry to an organization is the transition from educational establishment to the workplace. Most organizations lay on induction courses for their new recruits, which can last anything from half a day to several days. What is covered by these courses? A survey by the Industrial Society found that the most frequently cited objective of induction was to impart health and safety information – yes, health and safety information. Issues such as product or service information and understanding the climate and culture of the organization came nowhere.

The prevailing approach appears, in practice (and we present data at the end of this chapter which will shed light on this), to be one which assumes attendance on a course to be tantamount to 'being inducted'. This is the 'sheep dip' solution. Naturally, courses and workshops have a place in the induction process, but in isolation such courses can only provide an *introduction* to the organization, which is quite different to *induction*.

At its best, induction provides new recruits with a deeper understanding of the world they have just entered. Effective induction reduces the uncertainty they are likely to feel and clarifies for them their role in the business.

The benefits of a comprehensive induction programme can have far-reaching implications for both the business and the graduate (see Table 9.1). Four key issues need to be considered in the education-to-work transition process:

- levels of commitment and satisfaction
- culture change and shock
- how education prepares graduates for work
- expectations graduates and employers have of one another.

Table 9.1   The benefits of a good start

Benefits for graduates	Benefits for organizations
■ Positive attitude to the organization ■ Reinforcement of reason for joining ■ Better able to make an early contribution ■ Reduction of personal insecurity ■ Understanding performance standards	■ Positive attitude to the organization ■ Greater retention of recruits ■ Faster contribution

The best induction packages are those that can be tailored to meet individual needs. Induction should allow people to learn about themselves, the (real) organization structure, procedures and culture, and the job for which they have been recruited.

Levels of commitment and satisfaction

Commitment and satisfaction are key to a productive workforce. Amen to that. It follows that there is nothing more important than engaging trainees early on in their careers. And it turns out that the level of commitment and satisfaction graduates feel has a direct bearing on the contribution they make and how optimistic they are about their future relationship with their employer. Figure 9.1 illustrates graduates going from uninformed optimism through informed pessimism to hopeful realism and, finally, to informed optimism.

The first stage of the model is the typical honeymoon period that interns experience. As they settle in and begin to hear the corporate myths, the optimism begins to turn to pessimism. During this second stage they will also observe events which are contrary to their expectations. Once these negative aspects have surfaced, the challenge for the new recruit becomes how to understand and deal with this new corporate world. This period may also be accompanied by self-imposed under-utilization of the trainee's own talents.

As time goes by, trainees become increasingly acclimatized to their predicament, and they also begin to see some of their efforts come to fruition. This is stage 3 and it is critical, for one of the strongest influences

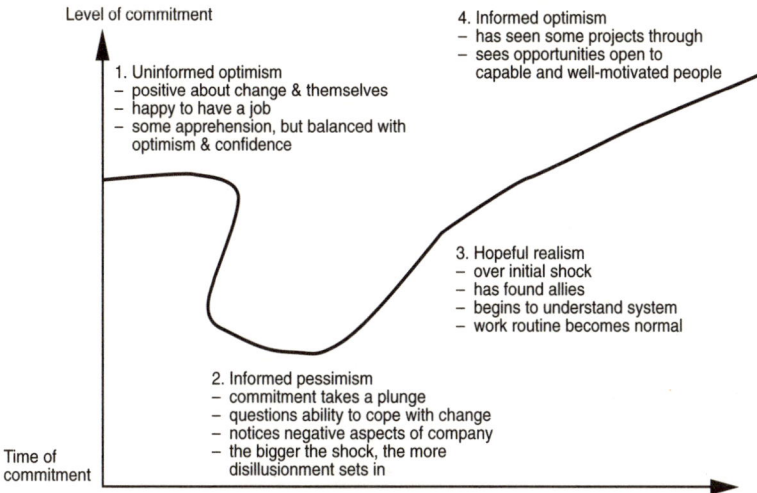

Level of commitment

1. Uninformed optimism
 – positive about change & themselves
 – happy to have a job
 – some apprehension, but balanced with
   optimism & confidence

4. Informed optimism
 – has seen some projects through
 – sees opportunities open to
   capable and well-motivated people

3. Hopeful realism
 – over initial shock
 – has found allies
 – begins to understand system
 – work routine becomes normal

2. Informed pessimism
 – commitment takes a plunge
 – questions ability to cope with change
 – notices negative aspects of company
 – the bigger the shock, the more
   disillusionment sets in

Time of
commitment

**Figure 9.1   The changing levels of commitment and optimism of
the trainee graduate**

on an individual's ability to contribute is their own confidence in their ability. As this confidence starts to develop, a new, more optimistic picture of their predicament emerges. It is at this final stage that the trainee is fully inducted and in a position to contribute to their full capacity.

The challenge for any graduate recruiter is to support the trainee through these stages and to move them on to stage 4 as swiftly as possible. But they must go through all four stages. Postponing the inevitable – the recruit seeing the company, warts and all – can have damaging effects on long-term attitudes toward the employer.

Culture change and shock

As soon as the graduate trainee sets foot in the building, they will be struck by a number of organizational characteristics – the clothes people wear, the degree of formality of the interactions between people, the friendliness of the reception and security staff, the office furniture, the use of colour, the amount and nature of company literature available. These and numerous other factors provide the individual with a set of clues as to how that organization operates, what approaches work there, and which ones are unlikely to work. Suddenly, all the individual's assumed modes of behaviour and action are called into question. Even relatively simple assumptions are tested, such as what clothes to wear, or how to address people.

All organizations have a raft of unspoken rules to which experienced people seem blissfully oblivious, and yet observe and respect, as they go about their business. You would think that the first order of business for a really useful induction programme would be to get these rules out into the open. But, of course, precisely because they are unspoken, no one wants to reveal what these rules are. Instead, new recruits are given a general explanation of policies and systems. Useful and necessary as this information is, this approach to induction – the factual, system-focused approach – often does little to reduce the uncertainty the graduate recruit is bound to be feeling.

Understanding the resident culture and what is expected in terms of behaviour and performance, is for many the key to success. Helping the new entrant to discover the 'unwritten rules' in an organization should be at the heart of any induction initiative.

How education prepares graduates for work

Some of the differences graduates will notice on entry into the workplace will be cultural, others will be practical. For example, the way reports are written in an academic setting is quite different to the way they are written in business. Similarly, activities such as meetings, teamworking and presentations all call for skills seldom called for or practised at college and university.

At the same time, graduates are now expected to add value from day one, to hit the deck running. The whole object is to minimize what has been called the 'time to talent'. The graduate, of course, experiences this as being thrown in at the deep end. Often there is insufficient time for development activities to occur. To be able to swim, recruits need to understand exactly what is required of them. A briefing, however comprehensive, is often insufficient. For many recruits, probably the most effective preparation is to be provided with examples of similar pieces of work. That way the intern becomes familiar with such subtleties as style and structure.

The issue here is less about imposing a style, more about providing a tangible indication of 'how things are done', in both the organization and the context of the generic 'workplace'. This type of support is critical, since it helps to reduce uncertainty and increases confidence and the likelihood of a positive outcome. Ultimately, it may even influence the value newcomers attach both to their own competence and to the organization.

Expectations graduates and employers have of each other

Everything we know tells us that one of the biggest barriers to a constructive relationship between employer and new employee is the expectation–reality gap. This is particularly the case with graduates. For them, their first job is the one which is going to launch them into a successful, potentially high-flying career. The employer has a different take on proceedings. Is this someone destined to sit in the boardroom? Or is it the supervisor of a team? Or is it neither of these, something less? And this is precisely the problem – differences in expectation.

Managing expectations must be an ongoing activity if the employer-graduate trainee relationship is to be harmonious, productive and lasting. It should also be explicit and honest. Both parties must be open about their own needs and about the opportunities they can offer. Without this honesty, the exercise is meaningless, and disillusion will set in. Essentially, the organization and graduate must negotiate a contract and then review and renegotiate it as appropriate.

In an attempt to manage expectations as openly as possible, many organizations are moving away from providing graduates with a vision of their future careers. Instead they are focusing on the notion of employ-ability. Phrases such as 'career development/progression', 'fast promotion' and 'job roles', are being replaced by 'accelerated development', 'learning opportunities' and 'supported development'. There has been a slow but sure acceptance by both employer and graduates that the contract is indeed changing. It is only with the acceptance and clarity of this key message that the graduate-employer relationship stands a chance.

What our research says

We sponsored two surveys. The first was a survey of graduate recruiters designed to uncover current practices used to induct graduates. Next, graduates were questioned to find out more about their perspectives on the practices used in their induction, their levels of knowledge about their work group, role and the culture of the organization, and their levels of commitment, satisfaction, intention to quit, and possibility of innovation in their job role. The data were collected using questionnaires between June and August 1999.

How organizations view induction

As Table 9.2 indicates, the main aim of induction, as organizations see it, is to introduce the organization's structure and clients. Introducing the culture comes some way behind. So induction is an exercise in knowledge imparting. Exactly how this is done is covered by Table 9.3. In fact, there are a number of avenues, all quite well used, with the company information pack – the knowledge – coming out on top.

Table 9.2   What organizations say are the most common aims of graduate induction

	Organizations with this aim (%)
1. To introduce the organization's structure and clients	34
2. To introduce the organization's culture	23
3. To build up the graduates' support networks	14
4. To develop future managers	13
5. To introduce graduates to a specific product or department	13

Table 9.3   The most common graduate induction practices used by organizations

	Organizations using this practice (%)
1. Company information packs	86
2. Interactions with peers	82
3. Formal on-site orientation sessions	77
4. Mentoring and/or sponsoring relationships	73
5. Immediate supervisors	66

To explore further what goes on, some induction tactics were defined:

- Collective – graduates are put through a set of common experiences.
- Investiture – the induction builds upon the entering traits and abilities of recruits.

- Sequential – the induction puts recruits through a specific sequence of steps before reaching their target roles.
- Fixed – the induction has a fixed timetable that is communicated to the recruits.
- Serial – the induction involves graduates being groomed into their roles by experienced organizational members such as senior managers.

The organizations in the sample were asked how far their induction activities involved these tactics. Table 9.4 has the results.

Table 9.4   Types of induction tactic used by companies

Induction tactic	Companies agreeing their induction involved this tactic (%)
Collective	71
Investiture	93
Sequential	75
Fixed	79
Serial	93

It seems that all these tactics are quite widely used. It is quite encouraging that induction appears to be tailored to individual skills and abilities (investiture), and that grooming, whatever that ultimately means, is commonplace (serial).

How graduates see the induction process

If we ask what the graduates themselves encounter, we see from Table 9.5 that they confirm the ubiquitous nature of the company information pack but that interaction with peers is not as common as the organizations themselves would like to believe. There is lots of pre-packed information, not so much meaningful interaction. It smacks of the health and safety approach to induction. A policy based on 'Read and go' is unlikely to be as effective as one which encourages interns to mingle with peers and more experienced colleagues.

Table 9.5   The most common induction practices encountered by graduates

	Graduates encountering this practice (%)
1. Company information packs	88
2. Formal on-site orientation sessions	81
3. Mentoring and/or sponsoring relationships	66
4. Interactions with peers	62
5. Off-site residential training	62

What induction tactics did interns encounter? Table 9.6 has the results.

Table 9.6   Types of induction tactic encountered by graduates

	Graduates agreeing their induction involved this tactic (%)
Collective	48
Investiture	81
Sequential	51
Fixed	66
Serial	75

So the recruits, too, recognize tailoring and grooming, if not as much as the employers claim is happening.

Table 9.7 shows how graduates would improve things.

Table 9.7   How graduates would improve induction

	Graduates suggesting these changes (%)
1. Better orientation to the organization and their role in it	11
2. More exposure to other departments	9
3. More structure to the induction programme	8
4. Less formal training courses	8

At the bottom line, how successful did the graduates polled think the induction had been in introducing them to *all* aspects of the organization? Table 9.8 has the data.

Table 9.8   How successful did graduates find their induction?

	Graduates (%)
Successful	58
Partially successful	22
Not successful	20

Actually, this is not such a bad outcome especially if it is reckoned that, for many, 'partially' might be quite good enough. You would expect more than one in five to complain if induction was going badly wrong.

General implications of the research

It appears that organizations can increase commitment and satisfaction among recruits, and decrease the intention to quit, by using a variety of induction tactics, especially individual tailoring of training and development, and grooming towards visible positions.

These are, however, quite conventional, even timid, tactics and are likely, in practice, to result in graduates adopting a somewhat traditional approach to work. Organizations may need to use other levers (such as creativity training, etc., not dealt with here) if they want to encourage innovative role orientations amongst their new graduates.

Key points from this chapter

- *Introduction* is quite different to *induction*. Courses which provide merely an introduction to an organization should not be mistaken for induction.
- At its best, induction provides new recruits with a deeper understanding of the world they have just entered.
- Induction should allow people to learn about themselves, the (real) organization structure, procedures and culture, and the job for which they have been recruited. Helping the new entrant to discover an organization's 'unwritten rules' should be at the heart of any induction initiative.
- Managing expectations must be ongoing if the employer–graduate trainee relationship is to be harmonious, productive and lasting.
- Commitment and satisfaction among recruits can be enhanced by using a variety of induction tactics, especially individual tailoring of training and development, and grooming towards visible positions.

After induction: managing, developing and retaining graduates

Getting graduates through the door is one thing: keeping them (providing you want to) is quite another. In this final chapter we discuss the way graduates are managed and how to increase the chances that you get the best from them. We look at these issues:

■ the manager-graduate relationship
■ developing graduates
■ retaining graduates.

Managing graduates

The manager–graduate relationship

The power a manager has over the graduate's ability to perform is immense. The manager must be (at least) all of the following:

■ A representative of the organization.
■ A role model.
■ A developer.
■ A champion.

The manager as representative of the organization
For many graduates entering the workplace, the manager *is* 'the company'. The new recruit will carefully observe the manager's behaviours and apparent attitudes and these will be interpreted as mirroring the organization's culture and values. It matters then that managers to whom new graduates are assigned are enthusiastic supporters of the business. Of course, enthusiastic support must be tempered with reality. Taken to the extreme, the unrealistically enthusiastic manager sows the seeds of later disappointment as the reality of the situation dawns on the newcomer.

The manager as role model

As the graduate becomes accustomed to the manager's behaviours and attitudes, the more he or she begins to adopt these very same behaviours and attitudes. This is where the graduate recruit differs from other newcomers. Being so new, and generally knowing so little of work, graduates are in the unique situation of being willing sponges to absorb what they witness on entry to the organization. What for the manager is personal style can take on a quite different significance for the new recruit, who might interpret it as the blueprint for managers in the company.

The manager as developer

Managers are in the unique position of being able to provide or withhold opportunities for graduates to test and develop their skills. The best managers will already have understood that the most satisfying entry to an organization occurs when the newcomer feels challenged, yet able to deliver.

Providing the right opportunities is only part of the story. Managers must tread a fine line between challenging graduates and guaranteeing them a safe environment. They should be skilled in giving the graduate honest and specific feedback – both positive and negative – at the same time facilitating the graduate's own awareness of their strengths and development needs. The manager must also be able to allow the graduate to fail and to learn from that failure without *feeling* a failure.

The manager as champion

Successful managers should expect to lose their trainee graduates to bigger and better things, both within and outside the organization. These will be the trainees who have developed to and beyond the expected standard. And these will be the managers – the champions – who have nurtured their graduates, supported their development, and provided opportunities for them to raise their profiles.

The graduate's manager can play a pivotal role in how the graduate performs and can influence their intention to remain with the organization. However, for managers to be able to play these roles, the organization must also shoulder some of the responsibility by ensuring that managers are equipped in terms of both skills and attitude to managing and developing graduates, and that they understand the parameters of their role as a 'graduate manager'. Finally, the need to provide an incentive for managers to execute their role effectively is critical. Recognizing the role for what it is is important, whether this be done by building it into the formal performance appraisal system or by being selective as to which managers are given the role.

Effective managers of graduates are likely to be:

■ well trained and experienced as managers/developers

- secure in their own ability to manage and in their position in the organization
- accountable for their responsibility to develop the graduate
- fully briefed on the recruitment objectives and strategy
- committed to and understanding of the development of graduates in the organization.

Developing graduates

The manager's role in developing the graduate is key. To managers falls the task of clarifying and structuring development processes so that new recruits are able to envisage where they go next.

The specific nature of development programmes will depend on many things, such as the type of business sector the organization operates in, professional developments and the position of the graduate. We consider four factors which will influence the general shape of development of graduates:

- the recruitment objectives and business strategy
- attributes and skills to be developed
- different approaches to graduate development schemes
- feedback.

Recruitment objectives and business strategy

Many businesses operate graduate development on a front-end basis, that is, they provide quick training to enable an immediate contribution. There is all too often a weak link between the strategic objectives of graduate recruitment and development and what actually happens in practice. For the successful development of graduates, businesses must ensure that the development programme is specifically tailored to the strategic objectives. Regular opportunities should be provided for trainees to discuss and explore their development needs. This dialogue should include discussion of the needs and wants of both employer and graduate as well as of the opportunities realistically on offer.

Skills to be developed

Recent graduates entering employment are likely to bring certain skills or strengths with them, yet they will require development in specific practical areas. This skills gap was emphasized earlier in Chapter 3 and it is hardly surprising when you consider the lack of work and 'life' experience that many graduates will have had. Core strengths and weaknesses customarily to be found in new graduates are summarized in Table 10.1.

Table 10.1   Strengths and development needs of recent graduates

Strengths	Development needs
■ Thinking skills ■ Up-to-date knowledge ■ Enthusiasm and energy ■ Willingness to learn' ■ Fresh and optimistic outlook ■ New ideas	■ Lack of work experience ■ Inability to communicate effectively ■ Lack of self-awareness ■ 'Superior attitude' ■ Lack of 'life experience'

In addition, there is a raft of transferable skills which need attention, such as financial skills, business awareness, sales/negotiating skills, management skills and written communication.

Graduates in technical roles particularly need these transferable skills. Clearly there is a gap that needs to be filled – development programmes and training are only effective if they manage to bridge this gap.

Graduates' own perceptions of their work-related competencies can also have implications for career planning and development. Graduates (and they are not alone in this) tend to rate themselves higher than their managers rate them. They feel confident about their interpersonal skills such as communication and conflict management, whereas their managers are much less convinced. Offering specific training in improving interpersonal skills and increasing self-awareness is a sensible course of action.

Five separate approaches to graduate development

It is possible to think of *five* separate approaches to graduate development.

- *General management schemes* – Programmes are usually four or more years in duration, and are aimed at a small number of graduates who are 'high flyers' – those who are thought to have great potential to be senior managers of the future.
- *Professional training schemes* – Programmes usually last about three years, and are aimed at incorporating formal study and practical work experience to enable graduates to undertake exams and obtain professional qualifications.

- *Medium-targeted schemes* – These schemes last between 18 and 36 months in duration, and are for graduates to develop in one particular function of an organization.
- *Short-targeted schemes* – Usually lasting less than eight months in duration these schemes are aimed at a basic level of training.
- *Direct job entry* – This development approach is basic, consisting of a personal development programme.

Regrettably, given the importance of development programmes, research has shown that most graduate development schemes are substandard. Most of the problems seem to stem from a lack of coordination between personnel functions, line managers and different departments or sites. The example below pinpoints aspects of good practice that ought to be incorporated into graduate development programmes.

Good practice in graduate development programmes

- Establish an overall corporate graduate policy with clear lines of management responsibility for its operation at different levels.
- Try not to create inflated expectations about jobs and career progress.
- Have an explicit rationale for the choice and sequencing of job placements on development schemes.
- Provide information for graduates to make career changes.
- Relate training to jobs.
- Monitor and record graduates' progress over time.
- Be flexible, as graduates will change with experience.
- The criteria for promotion should be made clear, and communicated to all.

The following case study examples of existing graduate development programmes illustrate the differences in development approaches.

The UK Police Force's Accelerated Promotion Scheme (APS)

Aim
The aim of this scheme is to attract and retain high-calibre individuals who want to join the police later in their careers, and to provide broader managerial and supervisory training and experience for those who have worked solely within the force. Every year between 30 and 40 exceptional UK police officers join the APS.

Content
Training is based on personal competencies which are defined on the basis of individual effectiveness. These include communication skills, problem-solving and decision-making skills, and sensitivity to the operating environment.

It is also based around organizational issues such as managing change, and organizational culture. Officers also spend time working in a non-police environment such as banking or retail.

The development scheme can take up to four years to complete, and is a sandwich course. After completing the course, candidates return for two further annual one-week courses to monitor their development.

Development in a large accountancy firm

Aim

The structure of graduate development in this organization is varied. A range of different training options is available, depending on the function and the geographical location of the office that a graduate joins. Various teams have been established to support graduates along their route.

Content

In one particular scheme, around 150 new graduates train together as a group for two years. In their third year, they go to an office of their choosing.

Various different teams have been established to support and help new graduates throughout their development. For example, there is a training development group (which formally organizes client contact for the graduate), an exam training group, a personal development team and a counselling manager team.

The organization also practises a 'buddy' process. Allocated to each graduate, a buddy is an individual who is one level above the graduate, from whom they can seek advice and talk with informally.

This organization clearly operates a mix of development activities which a graduate can pick and choose from, according to their own development needs, as well as the business' needs.

Feedback

A well-structured and planned graduate development programme will be quite ineffective if the scheme does not incorporate feedback. Regular, effective and constructive feedback has immense importance in the development of graduates. It is essential in enabling them to plot their own progress.

Some research found that there was a strong call from graduates for more frequent assessment. Most graduates are assessed annually, but would prefer to be assessed every six months.

The research also revealed that one-third of graduates had a mentor. Obtaining feedback and advice from a mentor can be particularly helpful, as graduates often want confidential support and advice from someone other than their manager. Feedback can also be effective coming from a third-party source – for example, from colleagues in a specific project team or department, or from a 'buddy'.

Mentoring

To see the terms 'coaching' and 'mentoring' used interchangeably is a common experience. True, there is a large overlap in the skills used by effective coaches and mentors, specifically in terms of providing the mentee (horrible word but what else?) with sufficient personal reflective space to think, understand and learn.

Is there a difference then? Perhaps it is best put this way. Mentoring involves some coaching, but a coach need not be a mentor: they are different relationships. A crucial difference between the two is that coaching involves the transfer of skill, plus some knowledge, and is mainly explicit. It is less about acquiring knowledge than acquiring the *skills* to apply knowledge. In contrast, mentoring focuses not on tasks or skills but on the transfer of *tacit knowledge,* or *wisdom*, which may include things like the politics of the job, and how to operate within the system and the rules without being unduly restrained by them, etc. Thus a key factor determining which is the most appropriate intervention is the nature of the learning which is to take place.

Mentoring is concerned with implications beyond the task, focuses on capability and potential rather than skills and performance, and is typically a longer-term relationship, often life-long, whereas coaching typically addresses a short-term need.

The agenda for mentoring is set by the learner, who also provides most of the feedback and reflection. A distinction can be made between career and developmental mentoring. The graduate will be looking for developmental mentoring.

Informal mentoring is unlikely to work because the structure and discipline to follow through will be absent. Better to formally appoint a developmental mentor whose functions will then be:

- Collaborating on tasks.
- Helping mentees set viable yet stretching personal goals.
- Challenging mentees to think more deeply about issues and themselves.
- Acting as a critical friend, honestly saying what others may be afraid to.
- Listening and questioning.
- Acting as a sounding-board for ideas and plans and giving constructive feedback.
- Explaining how the organization works, the politics, etc.
- Acting as a role model.
- Actively seeking out useful contacts for the mentee and advising on how to approach them.
- Stimulating mentees into making their own network connections.

Each relationship goes through different phases, which require slightly different emphasis and adjustment of behaviours:

1. Rapport-building – developing mutual trust and comfort
2. Direction-setting – setting goals for the relationship (these will evolve)
3. Progress-making – the most intensive stage, where experimentation and learning proceed rapidly

4. Maturation – when the relationship becomes more mutual in terms of learning and support, and the mentee becomes increasingly self-reliant

5. Closedown – when the formal relationship ends, often an informal continuity on an equal basis.

The mentor's role can thus be summarized as being both professional helper and supporter. It has been suggested that few mentors are comfortable with fulfilling both roles, as there is inevitably a degree of conflict, which is why the mentor should not be the immediate line manager, which would accentuate their role as assessor.

Mentoring as a purposeful development activity is often used for about 18 months. Formally bounded timescales are useful to ensure that good use is made of the time.

Retaining graduates

Ultimately an organization hopes to realize its investment in its graduates, in the form of a transition from graduate trainee to mature employee. Most organizations do not get a return on their money for at least two years. It has been estimated that the very 'best' organizations retain their graduates for at least two years while the 'worst' lose about a third in the first year and two-thirds by the third year. The worst organizations, therefore, make a net loss on their investment.

Of course one could counter this statement with the argument that most graduates take their first job with the intention of moving on after two or three years, after which organizations effectively trade their trainees for those from a comparable organization. In fact, most organizations seem happy to accept that their graduates' intention to leave increases as they approach the two-year point.

Ultimately, it comes back to an organization's recruitment strategy. If the intention was always to take on graduates into the 'mid-clerical' roles on the basis that the guaranteed intellect would add value to these roles, then swapping your graduates for someone else's, or even for completely untrained new graduates, is probably going to cause little disruption. On the other hand, if the recruitment strategy was to develop the big players of tomorrow, with the requisite investment in development, the loss is likely to be greater – both financially and practically. It is estimated that the management consultants Andersen Consulting invest £35,000 worth of training in each of their graduates over the first five years. That is a major investment to lose to your competitor.

Retaining graduates beyond the 'two-year itch'

Like selection, retention is a two-way process. The employer, in theory, chooses to retain the graduate, and the graduate chooses to remain with and contribute to the employer. Cranfield research, conducted over a six-year period, found that two years was generally seen as the watershed period for graduates in deciding whether to remain with or part from the organization.

What is interesting about this research is the apparent lack of responsibility taken by employers for the graduates who choose to leave. Managers tend to assume that those who leave the organization were in any case unsuitable, whilst those who remain are suitable. In essence, the employer's role in failing to retain the graduates who leave is largely dismissed, with responsibility for the breakdown of the relationship abdicated to the graduate. Some organizations are so lax with regard to the attrition of their graduates that they are not even aware who has left, let alone why.

Exit interviews, not surprisingly, appear to be rare and many organizations lack systems to formally track attrition/retention. On the whole, very little emphasis is placed on the collection of this information. Little wonder perhaps that managers view the attrition of graduates as an individual rather than a corporate issue.

If organizations are to retain their graduates – and their investment in them – they need to know why they are leaving. To assume that leaving the organization is solely the responsibility of the graduate and not that of the organization is itself an irresponsible line to take.

Causes of the 'two-year itch'

Why, as it happens, do graduates leave their first employer? If we can talk about a 'two-year itch', what causes it? Naturally there are no definitive answers to this question but varieties of disaffection among graduates have been noticed.

A big issue for graduates is how they will be absorbed into the organization. The fear is that having been treated initially as a favoured group they will then get lost along with everyone else. Or, at least, so it seems to them. Interestingly, the Cranfield research highlighted that many organizations now take the approach of not treating their graduates as a distinct population, preferring to focus on the overall development of the workforce. Given that graduates tend to nurture particular expectations of the organization on the very basis of their graduate status, this is a cause of insecurity.

Thus the complaint from graduates usually comes back to unmet promises and lack of clarity about their future career. Indeed, longitudinal research found that the longer a graduate stays with their employer, the more confusing prospects become. At least moving from company to company every two to three years provides a means of increasing their career dialogue with their employer.

The Cranfield research also identified a couple of themes pertinent to managing graduates' expectations. First, although some employers operated a 'high-potential' system, it was policy not to communicate this to their trainees. The rationale for steering away from overt labelling was to avoid raising false expectations. This was despite the existence in many of these organizations of covert labelling in the form of a database of high-potential trainees and an awareness of them amongst senior management. For these companies, keeping hold of high-potential trainees becomes less about offering a carrot, in the form of high expectations, and more about relying on managers and other reward systems to keep trainees engaged by what the company can currently offer.

Second, the research also found that four of the twenty companies included in its sample did not communicate clear expectations to its graduates. When taxed on this, the companies said that they themselves found it difficult to articulate clear statements of what it was that they expected of their graduate trainees, implying a lack of clear strategy on the part of these organizations.

Employers face a dilemma in how they manage their trainees. On the one hand, they are required to provide clear expectations that their graduates can get a hold on. On the other hand, they are rarely in the fortunate position of being able to predict the future, and hence cannot provide a clear development route for the trainee.

Perhaps employers should stay clear of providing rigid development systems, but instead provide a 'map of the terrain' for their trainees. This more fluid approach to managing expectations outlines the options available within the organization, whilst placing responsibility for getting there on the trainees. Ultimately the 'map' must be drawn by the employer's recruitment strategy and related objectives.

So it would seem that, whether or not employers intend it, graduates often feel as though they are left high and dry after around two years. This feeling, coupled with their initial high expectations on entry to the organization, creates a particular challenge to those employers whose recruitment strategy is to retain the talent they so recently recruited.

Key points from this chapter

■ Managers who are assigned responsibility for new recruits must be (at the very least), a representative of the organization, a role model, a developer and a champion.

■ The best managers understand that the most satisfying entry to an organization occurs when the newcomer feels challenged, yet able to deliver. The graduate must also be able to fail and to learn from that failure without *feeling* a failure.

■ Graduates are not as capable as they like to think they are, especially in the important areas of communication and interpersonal skills. Specific training should be offered in improving interpersonal skills and increasing self-awareness.

■ Most graduate development schemes are substandard, due to a lack of coordination between personnel functions, line managers, and different departments or sites.

■ Regular, effective and constructive feedback has immense importance in the development of graduates.

■ Obtaining feedback and advice from a mentor can be particularly helpful, as graduates often want confidential support and advice from someone other than their manager.

■ There is an (unfounded) assumption that those who leave the organization were in any case unsuitable, while those who remain are suitable. The attrition of graduates tends to be treated as an individual rather than a corporate issue.

■ Employers face a dilemma in trainee management: they are required to provide clear expectations that their graduates can get a hold on, while they are rarely in the fortunate position of being able to predict the future, and hence cannot provide a clear development route for the trainee.

Appendix
Best practice standards

To help you, we have summarized the ideas presented in the book into a set of 'Best Practice Guidelines'. These guidelines are intended to be used as a set of checklists against which you can benchmark your graduate recruitment processes.

Specifically, the guidelines cover:

■ taking a strategic approach
■ identifying your selection criteria
■ attracting a pool of suitable applicants
■ sifting/screening applications
■ choosing appropriate assessment methods
■ making the selection decision
■ monitoring the fairness and effectiveness of your recruitment procedure
■ inducting your graduates
■ developing your graduate trainees.

Taking a strategic approach

■ Graduate recruitment fits into an overall strategy for the business.
■ Senior management and HR understand how graduates are to be utilized.
■ The reasons for recruiting graduates, as opposed to other categories of applicant, have been thought through.
■ The organization knows the type of graduate recruiter it is, for example, a mass recruiter or a high-flyer recruiter.
■ Attraction and selection approaches align with the strategic approach to graduate recruitment.
■ The approach goes beyond recruitment to incorporate induction and development.

Identifying selection criteria

■ Selection criteria are developed for the different roles into which graduates are to be recruited.
■ All criteria can be justified in terms of the level and types of skills required for the different roles.
■ Criteria outline both qualifications and skills.
■ Criteria are written in clear unambiguous language.
■ Criteria reflect both the immediate and the longer-term needs of the business.
■ Criteria are checked for possible bias.

Attracting suitable applicants

Targeting the recruitment effort

■ A range of outlets/universities is used to attract a diverse pool of suitable graduate applicants.
■ Use graduate careers publications.
■ At presentations, use recent graduates to describe the organization.
■ Use a diverse set of presenters.
■ Encourage interaction with the students.
■ Be aware, always, of the type of image you want to project.
■ Tackle negative perceptions of the organization in the presentation.
■ Make inventive use of the Internet.

The graduate recruitment brochure

■ Clear and accurate descriptions of the roles are provided.
■ The rationale of selection criteria for different jobs is provided.
■ Selection criteria are clearly outlined.
■ The core values of the organization are outlined.
■ An insight into the organization's culture is provided.
■ Any case studies reflect a diverse set of people.
■ Student perceptions of the company, gained through the graduate brochure, are gathered to evaluate its success at conveying an appropriate image.
■ Brochures are designed in an engaging, reader friendly format.
■ Information is provided to help graduates 'self-select'.
■ Statements on equal opportunity should be included.

Consistency of recruitment and corporate image

- All information in the recruitment process is substantiated by the wider corporate image/presence in the market place.
- Espoused policies and values are seen to be practised by the organization at large, e.g. through its publicity, brand image, etc.
- All recruitment literature accurately reflects the company culture, values and business objectives.

Screening applications

Shortlist criteria

- The selection ratio should be established at the start of the exercise i.e. how many applicants is it practical to take through to the next stage?
- Shortlist criteria should reflect the key selection criteria which are essential to effective performance in the roles.
- All shortlisters are briefed and so have a common understanding of the criteria.

Application forms

- Application forms are designed around the selection criteria to encourage applicants to provide relevant information to be assessed.
- Application forms give clear guidance for completion.
- Application forms have a detachable monitoring form which is separated from the main form prior to screening.

Screening applications

- A marking scheme with clear guidance is provided to all shortlisters.
- All applications are processed in the same way.
- More than one person is involved in making shortlisting decisions.
- Candidates are shortlisted purely on the basis of how well they meet the selection criteria.
- Those with the highest ratings are invited for further assessment.
- Reasons for rejection or acceptance are recorded.
- Consistency/quality checks are built into the process.

Use of assessment methods

General guidelines

- All candidates are asked prior to attending the event if they have any specific requirements/needs.
- Where necessary, specific guidance is sought on candidate's special needs.
- Where candidates are travelling a distance to the event, overnight accommodation is offered.
- Everyone involved is thoroughly trained – administrators, interviewers, assessors, test users.
- Throughout the event a point of contact is made available to candidates, e.g. an administrator.

Interviews

- At least two interviewers are used or, for panel interviews, no more than four people.
- Interviews are structured around the selection criteria.
- Questions are designed to elicit specific evidence of candidate's proficiency on the selection criteria.
- Candidates are probed to give specific examples of what they have done in the past.
- Discriminatory questions and comments are avoided (e.g., marriage, family).
- The interview is used to gather information – decisions/ratings are made *after* the interview, not during it.
- Comprehensive notes are taken throughout the interview, and are kept on file for at least six months.
- All candidates are treated with dignity and respect, e.g. interviewers ensure all candidates begin and end the interview feeling comfortable with the process.
- Interviewers are fully briefed on the potential impact of their behaviour on candidates.

Practical exercises

- Candidates are advised in advance that practical exercises will form part of the assessment process.
- All practical exercises should be demonstrably related to the job.

- Exercises are designed around the selection criteria.
- Exercises are designed using specialist personnel advice.
- Exercises are pitched at the right level and are set in an appropriate context for the job.
- Assessors are provided with clear and comprehensive scoring guidelines for each exercise.
- Ratings are given on each selection criterion measured by the exercise.
- Evidence to justify ratings is written up for each criterion.

Tests and questionnaires

- Only tests and questionnaires that have been professionally produced and have evidence of being reliable, valid and fair are used.
- All tests are demonstrably related to specific selection criteria, i.e. job related.
- Tests are relevant to the job (content, level, timing).
- The content and pace of the test should not unjustifiably favour any particular group, e.g. on the basis of race or sex.
- Candidates are advised in advance that tests/questionnaires will be used and are sent preparation material in advance.
- All those involved in administering, scoring and interpreting tests and questionnaires are fully trained and registered.
- Appropriate norm groups are used to interpret test scores.
- Interpretations of personality measures are explored with candidates prior to making assessments.
- Test/questionnaire results are integrated with other sources of information.
- Tests/questionnaires are regularly reviewed to ensure they continue to assess characteristics related to the job.

Making the selection decision

Evaluation

- A rating scale with clearly defined anchors for each point are used.
- Each criterion is considered separately and assigned an overall rating.
- Evidence for all ratings, on all criteria, is discussed and agreed.
- Guidance, e.g. a decision table, is provided for recruiters to assign an overall recommendation.
- Decisions are based upon more than one source of information.
- The successful candidates are those who match most closely the criteria.

■ Reasons for rejection/acceptance are recorded and kept on file for at least six months.

Use of references

■ References are used as a secondary source of information only.
■ References are used to check information which is factual and objective.
■ If information of a more judgemental nature is necessary to supplement assessment information, specific questions should be asked and evidence elicited to back up judgement.

Feedback

■ Opportunities for feedback should be given to all candidates, whether successful or unsuccessful.

Monitoring your recruitment procedure

Collecting information

■ At a minimum, information on candidates' sex, race, age and disability is collected at each stage of the selection process.
■ Information on candidates' scores is collated on a central database.
■ Candidates (successful and unsuccessful) are randomly canvassed to gain their perceptions of each stage of the recruitment process in terms of:
  – fairness
  – extent to which the event represented the job/company
  – level of difficulty
  – smoothness of the administration.
■ Performance information for successful candidates is periodically collected.

Evaluating fairness and effectiveness

■ Information is analysed to identify proportions of different groups (e.g. gender, ethnicity, institution, disability, etc.) present at each stage of the recruitment process, from requesting an application form to accepting/refusing an offer of employment.

■ Recruitment and selection data are monitored regularly to check for evidence of adverse impact. This includes ethnic origin, gender and disability, as a minimum.
■ Periodic checks are made for a positive statistical relationship between performance on elements of the recruitment process and performance in the job.
■ Information on perceptions of the recruitment process are reviewed to identify areas for improvement.
■ The selection criteria and elements of the procedure (e.g. interview, exercises, tests, etc.) are regularly qualitatively reviewed to check for their continued relevance to:
  – the business strategy and objectives
  – the jobs/roles being recruited for
  – the context of the jobs
  – level of difficulty/complexity in the job.
■ Quality checks are periodically conducted to check interviewers'/ assessors' evidence against ratings/recommendations.
■ Follow-up action is taken in response to the results of monitoring and is reviewed.

Inducting your graduates

Before the graduate joins

■ Practical help is offered to graduates relocating to the area.
■ Key information about the job and company is sent in advance to the new recruit.
■ The recruit is informed of any major changes prior to joining.
■ A key contact is allocated to every recruit should they have any queries or need help.
■ Projects are outlined in advance to be passed to the recruit on arrival.
■ Careful consideration is given to allocation of managers to recruits.
■ Graduates' managers are fully briefed and prepared for their role.

On joining

■ Induction covers practical issues, legislative issues, relevant procedures, structure and the corporate culture.
■ Information provided at induction gives recruits a realistic view of the organization.

- Recruits are provided with a framework which they can use to find out the information they need to know (e.g. induction interview project).
- Induction is not perceived to be a one-off event, but an ongoing process lasting up to six months.
- Graduates' managers play a key role in their graduates' induction.
- Managers provide their recruits with a clear understanding of their role, objectives and how they fit into the structure.
- Graduates are assigned an experienced 'buddy' to help them find their way around the organization (physically and metaphorically!).
- New recruits are given opportunities to contribute at an early stage.
- Regular opportunities are provided for graduates to review their progress with their manager.

Developing your graduate trainees

- Information from the recruitment event is used as a basis for a discussion of development needs.
- Development programmes are aligned to the business strategy/objectives.
- All recruits construct a development plan (including SMART objectives, actions and timescales) with their manager.
- Regular reviews are scheduled to assess progress and explore new development needs.
- Managers are skilled to provide clear, constructive feedback on performance.
- All graduates know who to contact for advice on their development.
- A range of methods are used to provide development opportunities (e.g. courses, on-the-job coaching, etc.).
- Development focuses on both the current role and potential future roles.
- A central person is allocated responsibility for tracking graduates' development.

Further reading and online viewing

Further reading

For the original Pearn Kandola research see: (1) Whiddett, S., Payne, T. and Kandola, R., 'Organisational preference: are public and private sector organisation perceived differently as potential employers?', *BPS Occupational Psychology Book of Conference Proceedings*, 1995, 205–211. (2) Keane, C. and Kandola, R. 'But they just don't apply', *BPS Occupational Psychology Book of Conference Proceedings*, 1998 5–8. Jane Beresford's research (Chapter 9) is written up in her MSc thesis, Institute of Work Psychology, University of Sheffield, 1999.

Bracken, D. W., *Should 360-degree Feedback be Used Only for Developmental Purposes?*, Greensboro, NC: Center for Creative Leadership, 1997.

Clutterbuck, D., *Learning Alliances*, London: IPD, 1998.

Cranfield University, *What is on offer? The graduate career challenge*, Cranfield: Human Resource Research Centre, 1995.

Daniels, L. and McGarraher, L., *Work-life Manual*, Glasgow: Industrial Society, 2000.

Employee Development Bulletin, *Mentoring in effective staff development*, London: IRS, 1998.

Employee Development Bulletin, *The state of selection: an IRS survey*, London: IRS, 1997.

Hampden-Turner, C. and Trompenaars, F., *The Seven Cultures of Capitalism*, London: Piatkus, 1994.

Herriot, P. and Pemberton, C., *New Deals – The Revolution in Managerial Careers*, Chichester: Wiley, 1995.

Hobson's, *Equal Opportunity Casebook: Ethnic Minority Graduates and Their Careers*, London: Hobson's, 1997. Hobson's publishes its *Equal Opportunities Casebook* annually, as well as guides and casebooks for graduates, disabled and ethnic minority trainees, and others.

Holbeche, L., *High Flyers and Succession Planning in Changing Organisations*, Roffey Park, Susex: Roffey Park Management Institute, 1998.

Income Data Services, *Management Pay Review's fourteenth survey of graduate pay and progression*, February 2000 – see IDS website <www.incomesdata.co.uk>.

Industrial Society, *Induction: Managing best practice*, Issue 10, 1995.

Jones, T., *Britain's Ethnic Minorities*, London: PSI, 1993.

Kandola, R. S. and Fullerton, J., *Diversity in Action*, London: IPD, 1998.

McCall, W., *High Flyers: Developing the Next Generation of Leaders*, Cambridge, MA: Harvard Business School Press, 1998.

Pearn Kandola, *Tools for assessment and development centres: A set of tools for practitioners produced by Pearn Kandola*, London: IPD, 1996.

The Times Top 100 Graduate Employers, London: High Flier Publications Ltd, 1999.

Trompenaars, F., *Riding the Waves of Culture*, London: Economist Books, 1993.

UCAS (Universities and Colleges Admissions Services), *What do graduates do? 2000*, Cheltenham: UCAS Enterprises, 1999.

UCAS statistics, published April 14 and May 26, 2000 – see UCAS website <www.ucas.ac.uk>.

Whiddett, S. and Hollyforde, S., *The Competencies Handbook*, London: IPD, 1999.

Wood, R. and Payne, T., *Competency-Based Recruitment and Selection*, Chichester: Wiley, 1998.

Online viewing

The American Institute for Managing Diversity at www.aimd.org
Association of Graduate Recruiters at www.agr.org.uk
British Psychological Society at www.bps.org.uk
Center for Creative Leadership at www.ccl.org
Commission for Racial Equality at www.cre.gov.uk
Graduate facts at www.campus.monster.co.uk
Graduate high flyer vacancies at www.high-flyers.co.uk
Gradunet's virtual careers online at www.gradunet.co.uk
Higher education statistics agency at www.hesa.ac.uk
Hobson's global careers and education service at www.hobsons.co.uk
Incomes Data Services at www.incomesdata.co.uk
Institute of Personnel and Development at www.ipd.co.uk
Managing diversity newsletter at www.jalmc.org/mg-diver.htm
The milkround online at www.milkround.com
Oxford Psychologists Press at www.opp.co.uk
Pearn Kandola at www.pearnkandola.com
Roleplay actors at www.roleplayuk.com

Saville and Holdsworth at www.shlgroup.com
Training and induction services – graduate link at www.pwcglobal.com.
Universities and Colleges Admissions Services at www.ucas.ac.uk

Index